1892–1941

Марина Цветаева

SOUL AND PASSION:
Marina Tsvetaeva's Classical Plays
Second Edition

Introduction, Translation, and Notes
by
Zara Martirosova Torlone
and
Maria Stadter Fox

Oxford, Ohio
Staroe Vino

CONTENTS

ACKNOWLEDGMENTS

We are grateful to the friends, colleagues, and students who have been kind enough to express interest in this project during its long gestation.

In particular, I would like to thank the following people: Madeline Levine, for first giving me Tsvetaeva's *Teatr* many years ago; Domnica Radulescu and the participants of several meetings of the National Symposium of Theater in Academe at Washington & Lee University, for their heartening interest in both Tsvetaeva's *Phaedra* and my own progress with the translation; Zara M. Torlone, for the impetus and the energy to pursue publication, as well as good advice on difficult passages; my father, Philip A. Stadter, for a careful and helpful reading of a late draft of the translation; and finally, my family, for their support and encouragement.

M. S. F.

I would like to thank: my students at Miami University of Ohio for their kind encouragement as they read the first versions of my translation of *Ariadne*; Maria Stadter Fox for her numerous readings and corrections of my translation; my father Dr. Sergey Martirosov who introduced me to Tsvetaeva's poetry when it was still a "forbidden fruit" in Soviet Union; my mother, Samvelina Pogosova, for her meticulous editing; Evan Hayes for preparing this edition for publication; my husband Mark and my daughters, Christina and Francesca, for their patience and love.

Z. M. T.

Translators' Note

The main purpose of this edition is to bring to the Anglophone reader the classical plays of Marina Tsvetaeva, one of the most important and influential Russian poets of the twentieth century. We have had in mind primarily three readerships: the student of a discipline other than the study of Russian literature; the general reader; and the student of Russian who may need some help with reading Tsvetaeva. Therefore, we have aimed at staying faithful to the original Russian texts without sacrificing the complexity of the verse and idiom, which present substantial challenges in translation.

The present Russian texts of *Ariadne* and *Phaedra* are based on the texts of the plays presented in volume 5 of Tsvetaeva's *Stikhotvorenija i poemy v pjati tomakh* edited by Alexander Sumerkin. Every effort has been made by the translators to contact the rights holders of the Russica Publishers edition of the Russian texts of *Ariadna* and *Phaedra*.

Occasionally Sumerkin's edition differs from that of *Teatr*, edited by Ariadna Efron and Anna Saakjants; while Sumerkin's text has been preferred, Efron and Saakjants's reading is given in the notes when it seemed of interest to the non-specialist. The reader of Russian may wish to consult these editions, as they contain material about the plays from Tsvetaeva's own notebooks and letters. We omit Tsvetaeva's own notes for the plays, which are primarily about word stress and pronunciation, as we did not consider them useful for readers of this edition.

Maria Stadter Fox would like to acknowledge the following translations as being helpful while working on her own:

Cvetaeva, Marina. Ariane: *Tragédie de Marina Cvetaeva traduite et commentée.* Edited and translated by Rose Lafoy. Clermont-Ferrand: Faculté des Lettres et Sciences Humaines de l'Université de Clermont-Ferrand, 1981.

Cvetaeva, Marina. *Fedra / Fedra*. Bilingual edition. Translated and edited by Luisa de Nardis. Biblioteca di cultura 403. Rome: Bulzoni Editore, 1990.

Cvetaeva, Marina. *Arianna / Ariadna*. Bilingual edition. Translated and edited by Luisa de Nardis. Biblioteca di cultura 439. Rome: Bulzoni Editore, 1991.

Tsvétaeva, Marina. *Phèdre*. Translated by Jean-Pierre Morel. Les belles infidèles. Arles: Actes Sud, 1991.

NOTE to the SECOND EDITION

In September 2018, CreateSpace announced it would merge with KDP, another Amazon publishing division. All books published through CreateSpace would be moved over to KDP. Unfortunately, KDP does not support the Cyrillic alphabet.

We regret that this second edition does not have the facing Russian text as in the original edition.

Maria Stadter Fox
Zara Martirosova Torlone

September 2018

INTRODUCTION: *Soul and Passion*

Marina Ivanovna Tsvetaeva's (1892-1941) interest in classical myth was evident from her first collections of poems. Her use of classical references matured especially in *Remeslo* (*Craft*, 1922) and in her collection *Posle Rossii* (*After Russia*, 1923); the characters taken from classical mythology are chosen not at random but in connection with the central preoccupations of Tsvetaeva's poetic system. It comes therefore as no surprise that around the same time (1923) Tsvetaeva began working on her classical dramas.

Her interest in classical drama stemmed from different concerns than those of her Russian predecessors in mythological tragedy, Vyacheslav Ivanov (1866-1949) and Innokenty Annensky (1856-1909).[1] While Ivanov and Annensky strove to display the confidence and knowledge of classical scholars in their classical dramas, Tsvetaeva portrayed herself as someone with only superficial, if any, knowledge of her classical sources.[2] Tsvetaeva always downplayed her direct knowledge of antiquity. Nevertheless, she grew up in the household of Professor Ivan Tsvetaev, whose major success was the foundation of the Museum of Fine Arts, today known as the Pushkin State Museum of Fine Arts.[3] Therefore one must question Tsvetaeva's own flippant admittance of ignorance. The daughter of Ivan Tsvetaev and a close friend of the classical philologist Vladimir Nilender (1883-1965), who published his translation of Heraclitus in 1910 (the year Marina met him), she most likely had more than a passing acquaintance with classical tragedy (Nilender later also translated Aeschylus and Sophocles). In her letters to Alexander Bakhrakh in 1923 she admitted that she was avidly reading the Greeks ("I cannot read anyone except the Greeks") and she asked him for a copy of Nietzsche's *The Birth of Tragedy*.[4] Tsvetaeva's disingenuousness in asserting her independence from any sources is also evident in her letter to Yury Ivask in which she also denied any indebtedness to Ivanov: "I have never been under the influence of V. Ivanov – nor of anyone at all").[5] In one of her letters Tsvetaeva even went so far as to call Ivanov "a pseudoclassicist," an attack that demonstrated her insistence on emulation rather than imitation of any source.[6]

While both Ivanov and Annensky were the most erudite classical scholars on the Russian cultural landscape, Tsvetaeva's use of classical sources in the creation of her mythological dramas was limited, by her own assertion, to the didactic, moralizing adaptation of Greek myths by Gustav Schwab, *Die schönsten Sagen des klassischen Altertums*, published in 1837-9 and written for German children of the Victorian era.[7] Although most scholars agree that this bowdlerized adaptation of Greek myths is the main source of Tsvetaeva's mythics, again, her denial of any knowledge of ancient sources must be taken with a grain of salt. Tsvetaeva may have been unwilling to admit that she had read and absorbed (albeit in translation) Euripides', and perhaps Catullus's and Seneca's, renditions of the myth of Theseus due to her conscious and aggressive desire to set herself apart from her Russian predecessors in mythological tragedy. Her choice of plots is a refreshing change from Ivanov's and especially Annensky's obsessive interest in the *arcana* of classical mythology and in assuming the role of a mythographer. Furthermore, "her source-based works frequently alluded – implicitly or explicitly – to familiar, traditional treatments of canonical material."[8] Tsvetaeva's interest in Greek myth and tragedy was not scholarly; it was personal and strongly related to circumstances of her life, and intertwined with the rest of her poetics.

Another reason for her self-professed predilection for German sources was Tsvetaeva's lifelong fondness for German Romanticism. An avid reader of the German Romantics (Heine, Novalis, Bettina von Arnim, and Goethe), Tsvetaeva might have absorbed some of her classical mythology through these authors as well as through the German anthologies of Schwab and Stoll.[9] In her 1919 essay *"O Germanii"* ("On Germany") Tsvetaeva writes:

> I might be saying something bizarre, but for me Germany is Greece continued, ancient, and youthful. The Germans are the heirs. And not knowing Greek, I will not accept from anybody's hands, from anybody's lips but the German that nectar, that ambrosia.[10]

Considering this interest in the German reception of antiquity, it is understandable why, in writing her classical tragedies, Tsvetaeva was interested in Nietzsche's *The Birth of Tragedy*, which probably influenced her conception of Bacchus in *Ariadne*.[11]

All of Tsvetaeva's poetry is inextricably connected with her biography and her binary perception of the world. One of the most important binary oppositions in Tsvetaeva's poetry is that of masculine and feminine.[12] This opposition is obvious in her lyric poetry and in her longer poems based on Russian folk tales, such as *Tsar'-Devitsa* (*The Tsar-Maiden*), which tells the story of a lecherous old Tsar, his beautiful second wife, and her desire for her stepson. The struggle between masculine and feminine, the unavailable object of passion, and the theme of *eros-nosos* ("love-sickness") reappear in Tsvetaeva's classical tragedies, fueled by the sweeping strength of personal emotion, rather than in reflection of ideological and philosophical views, as in the work of her Russian predecessors.

Tsvetaeva had a long-standing interest in playwriting as "a new ... means of expressing human interrelations, conflicts, characters and passions."[13] In 1918 she grew increasingly close to a group of actors in the Third Studio of the Moscow Art Theater and wrote her six "romantic" plays with several of the actors in mind. None of these plays, which were completed in 1918-19, was ever performed during her lifetime and, although her interest in drama continued, Tsvetaeva articulated rather vocally her dislike for the theater. She included her opinion on theater in the preface to her play *Konets Kazanovy* (*The End of Casanova*) published in 1922, stating categorically:

> I do not respect Theater, I am not attracted to Theater, and I do not reckon with Theater ...
> But the essence of the Poet – is to believe in the word!
> ...
> Theater I always feel as a violence.
> Theater is the destruction of my solitude with the Hero, solitude with the Poet, solitude with the Dream – the third player at a love rendezvous.
> ...

"And yet you write plays!" – This is not a play, this is a *poèma* -
simply love: Casanova's thousand and first declaration of love.
This is [just as much] theater, as I – am an actress.
Anyone who knows me will smile.[14]

Tsvetaeva directs the reader to interpret her classical plays, then, in the
same vein as the *End of Casanova*, not as dramas intended for a stage or as
part of any literary movement like the Slavonic Renaissance of the
Symbolists, but as a continuation of the main preoccupations of
Tsvetaeva's poetics.

Tsvetaeva discovered her dramatic voice at the same time and
even earlier than the European writers who were also breathing fresh life
into Greek tragedy. Jean Cocteau wrote *Antigone* in 1922 and *Orphée* in
1926, while Jean Giraudoux's *Amphitryon* did not appear until 1929, and
Jean Anouilh's *Antigone* as well as Jean-Paul Sartre's *Les mouches* not until
1942 and 1943 respectively. W. B. Yeats wrote his *Sophocles' King Oedipus* in
1928 and *Sophocles' Oedipus at Colonus* in 1934, while T. S. Eliot began his
use of Greek plots for a modern audience only in 1939. Tsvetaeva was
decisively one of the pioneers in creating original neo-classical tragedies
with a pronounced and explicitly articulated twentieth-century sensibility,
which centered on the exploration of a dialectic between the main
generative oppositions in her poetics: male and female.

"Theseus": Trilogy Interrupted

While in emigration she wrote two tragedies, *Ariadne* (1927) and
Phaedra (1928), and meant to write a third, *Helen*. The trilogy was originally
entitled "Wrath of Aphrodite" but was later renamed, more simply,
"Theseus."[15] She explains her interest in the Theseus myth in a letter to a
friend:

> Did you know that all women fell to Theseus's lot, all-forever?
> Ariadne (soul), Antiope (Amazon), Phaedra (passion), Helen
> (beauty). That Trojan Helen. The seventy-year-old Theseus
> abducted her when she was seven years old and died because of
> her.
>
> So many loves and *all* unhappy. The last is the worst of all,
> because he loved a doll...[16]

It is unfortunate that Tsvetaeva never wrote the third part of the trilogy: one would like to have seen how she imagined the relationship between the old hero and the fatally beautiful child. The two extant plays, however, offer an extraordinary range and depth of poetic power and mastery.

"In the creation of a contemporary work on a mythological theme," writes Tomas Venclova in his discussion of Russian mythological tragedy, "a double transition takes place: from the language of myth into the language of art and from the language of an ancient (classical or other) culture into the language of modern culture. It is rather difficult in practice to distinguish these processes."[17] While Ivanov and Annensky tried to rethink Greek tragedy in modern terms, each following their chosen Greek model, Tsvetaeva was doing the same in personal terms applicable to the rest of her poetics at that time. The theme she aimed to explore in the trilogy was the fatal and doomed but true passion of love. Tsvetaeva's uncanny penchant for selecting unavailable and sometimes unworthy lovers was translated into Theseus's passion for Ariadne, Ariadne's for Theseus, and Phaedra's for Hippolytus. In that respect Tsvetaeva was not much different from her ancient predecessors, at least in Latin poetry, who found the myths about Cretan women especially attractive because of "the voicing of feminine passion."[18]

Ariadne: Abandoned or Conceded?

Ariadne (*Ariadna*) was intended as the first play of the unfinished trilogy.[19] The play consists of five scenes (tableaux) that retell the familiar myth about Ariadne's assistance of Theseus and her subsequent abandonment by him on the island of Naxos. It is clear from Tsvetaeva's treatment of the characters that she could not have been solely dependent on Schwab since in that source Theseus is presented as the epitome of heroic behavior, a role model for the young. Tsvetaeva's Theseus is irrational, often foolish in his single-minded desire for heroic glory, and yearning for combat. His thoughts before entering the labyrinth are not of the loss of young life or of his old father but the self-absorbed musings of an immature youth; they are not, however, altogether incongruous with his ambition to be remembered as a great hero. Tsvetaeva emphasizes his legendary forgetfulness but casts it in a different light. More importantly, Tsvetaeva's Theseus undergoes an evolution as the play progresses:

immature at first, he eventually comes of age when he chooses to part with his love, making a choice in which neither alternative is unambiguously positive.

By the same token Tsvetaeva's Ariadne is also much more complex than the bowdlerized version in Schwab. Her decision to sail with Theseus is burdened with proleptic premonitions bordering on divine vision.[20] Since her only meaningful earthly relationship, with her father Minos, is one of insecurity and uncertainty because he longs for a son, she anticipates that Theseus will be weak in the realm of emotions as well. While Ariadne, for the most part, fulfills the expectation of the traditional demure female (at least in comparison with her sister Phaedra), she also understands the consequences of her choice when she decides to follow Theseus and leave her homeland. Not yet fully developed into a tragic heroine (as Phaedra is) she nonetheless reflects Tsvetaeva's main preoccupation in the trilogy: unhappy love. It is, however, the *agōn* (or sharp conflict expressed in debate) between Bacchus and Theseus that recalls ancient tragedy most strikingly and forms the culmination of the play.

Theseus's abandonment of Ariadne is of pivotal interest for Tsvetaeva's dramatic action and "modernization" of the play.[21] She treats the event, drawn from her acknowledged source, Schwab, in an unusual way. Schwab himself follows the less well-known rendering of Diodorus Siculus,[22] borrowing the episode of the dream in which Bacchus appears to Theseus and scares him into abandoning Ariadne. In that version fear is the primary reason for Theseus's treacherous conduct, which even Schwab acknowledges to be lacking in heroic honor.[23] Tsvetaeva, however, alters significantly the confrontation between Bacchus and Theseus over the body of the sleeping Ariadne by turning it into the *agōn* at the core of the tragic conflict, as much a struggle between two rival lovers as it is a matter of general and social import. Tsvetaeva explicates the confrontation between Bacchus and Theseus in the outline in her notebook from November 1923 as follows:

Dialogue between Dionysus and Theseus. To *understand* Dionysus: does he want merely Ariadne or immortality for her? Who is more magnanimous: Theseus or the god? Dialogue over her sleeping. Theseus's doubts: but maybe earth is worth the sky? -- Yes, especially when these cheeks become earth! I cannot become a

man, you become a god. (I cannot become less, you become --
more!). [24]

These preliminary notes find their elaboration in the culminating scene,
with one added feature reflected in the final line of her notes of August
1924: "It is nothing to slay the Minotaur, but there is a monster most
horrible: your own greedy heart: slay that!" [25]

Tsvetaeva's Theseus, unlike his ancient counterparts, is at first
reluctant to give Ariadne up and is fearless when faced with the divine
presence. Furthermore, he juxtaposes the intensity of his mortal passion
with the ephemeral promise of the god's affection. Although Theseus's
arguments sound persuasive, Bacchus prevails, not because his love for
Ariadne proves stronger, but because Theseus comes to realize that he
cannot give Ariadne one thing Bacchus can: immortality. Theseus in the
end acknowledges his powerlessness and his *hubris*[26] in face of the divine
and admits the fleeting nature of the happiness he can offer to Ariadne.
The abandonment of Ariadne becomes in Tsvetaeva's rendering a heroic
endeavor, a rational and even selfless choice signifying the maturity of the
hero. Theseus's subsequent forgetfulness and guilt in the death of his own
father are explained as the result of his grief over the loss of Ariadne rather
than as a moral failure to fulfill his promises.

The most astonishing feature of Tsvetaeva's tragic plot in *Ariadne*,
however, is the absence of Ariadne's voice after her abandonment.
Tsvetaeva decides her fate in the play through the debate of two male
protagonists over her sleeping body.[27] The heroine receives her final
apotheosis without desiring it, although she foresees it in her exchange
with Theseus before her departure from Crete, when she cites the dangers
of divine love for "mortal maidens."[28] The elevation of Theseus to tragic
status also illustrates Tsvetaeva's idealization of the male protagonist, who
despite his questionable conduct is still portrayed as a hero torn between
passion and fate.

The binary opposition between male and female is decided in the
first play of the trilogy in favor of the male protagonist: he is enabled to
make the choice, while she plays the silent or rather enabling role. In that
role Ariadne is deprived of the full range of character typical of tragic
Greek heroines, such as Clytemnestra, Helen, Phaedra, Medea, or
Antigone, whose male antagonists yield and are sacrificed to the intensity
of the women's desires or hatred. Although Ariadne is Aphrodite's

favorite, she is undone by her desire for an ordinary woman's fate: a husband and children. When she is given the chance to articulate her feelings (as late in the play as the third tableau), she argues powerfully that she cannot follow Theseus because that will lead to unhappiness for both of them. But her strong argumentation is interrupted by the chorus of Athenian youths and maidens saved by Theseus from the Minotaur. One stanza by the chorus in particular counters all of Ariadne's good reasoning and explains her fatal choice and her later muteness in the play: "I will be beloved / And a wife / And I will rock my children to sleep."[29] Ariadne's resistance to Theseus vanishes as she contemplates that ordinary happiness and she decides, against her best judgment, to follow Theseus. At the moment she agrees to go with Theseus, Ariadne finally gives him her name — the first time her name is spoken in the play (earlier references have been "daughter," "virgin," etc.). It is the last word she says while awake. When she gives him her name, she seems to surrender herself and her future as well. Ariadne's successor in Theseus's affections, Phaedra, is instead a tragic heroine able to voice her passion and her sorrow in her own right.

Phaedra: *Speaking Up*

Tsvetaeva's *Phaedra (Fedra)*, the second play of the trilogy, must be considered a continuation of the lyric cycle written in March of 1923 and also entitled *Phaedra*. The first poem of the cycle, entitled *"Zhaloba"* ("Complaint"), is a description of the physical pain inflicted on Phaedra by her passion for her stepson. Here the description of Phaedra's love has familiar Euripidean overtones of "love-sickness" complete with fever and outright physical pain. The second poem of the cycle, *"Poslanie"* ("A Letter"), written in the form of a letter from Phaedra to Hippolytus, continues the theme of unrequited passion. The connection between physical desire and the longing of the soul is especially striking in this poem, in which the spiritual consummation of love becomes intertwined with physical consummation. Hippolytus is again described as the beloved, not the lover, a passive recipient of Phaedra's devouring emotions. That Phaedra identifies herself also as a rider or horsewoman ("*ja naezdnitsa* tozhe")[30] shows that Tsvetaeva was a careful reader of Euripides. In Euripides' *Hippolytus*, the love-sick Phaedra searches for the space where her union with Hippolytus would be natural.[31] Tsvetaeva's

Phaedra, like Euripides' heroine, wants to become an Amazon, the only type of woman Hippolytus, named after his mother the Amazon Hippolyta (also known as Antiope), does not despise.[32] All these themes of the lyric cycle *Phaedra* resonate through the second play of the "Theseus" trilogy.

Tsvetaeva's tragedy *Phaedra* consists of four scenes and has far fewer characters than *Ariadne*: Phaedra, Hippolytus, Theseus, the Nurse, and the Servant. The action of the play is set in Troezen where Theseus has brought his young wife Phaedra to visit his adult son Hippolytus. The opening chorus of Hippolytus's huntsmen echoes both Hippolytus's first entrance in Euripides' *Hippolytus* and his misogynistic monologue later in the ancient play.[33] In his first appearance, Euripides' Hippolytus emphasizes his vow of chastity as he sings his hymn to Artemis; in the second, he condemns "woman's wickedness" and declares in a somewhat exaggerated manner his hatred for the whole female sex.[34] The first monologue of Tsvetaeva's Hippolytus, which immediately follows the chorus, is, however, far from the self-assured and slightly arrogant Euripidean version. He describes his dream of ill omen in which his wounded dead mother appears to him. Hippolytus is troubled by the dream and his friends try to offer him consolation. Soon after, Phaedra appears and the two of them reveal their identities, he as a worshipper of Artemis, she as a servant of Aphrodite. The divine juxtaposition familiar from Euripides is thus established here also.

The second scene finds Phaedra sick with love, while her maidservants question the nature of her sickness. Here the importance of the character of the Nurse in the play becomes manifest. The Nurse, unlike Phaedra, is thrilled rather than shocked by Phaedra's eventual confession of love for Hippolytus. She, living vicariously through Phaedra's passion, insists that it must be consummated. The physical imagery in the speech of the unlovable old Nurse is striking in its stark description of sexual desire.[35] To prove her point that love should be more powerful than any other loyalty, she even somewhat illogically invokes the fate of all of Phaedra's ill-fated female relatives. The same recounting of Phaedra's female relatives' ill-fated loves appears in Euripides' play.[36] While Schwab's rendition of the story (although based largely on Euripides' play) omits any reference to Pasiphae and her unconventional progeny since his versions were intended for educating young people, Euripides uses the reference to Phaedra's mother to imply hereditary necessity in choosing forbidden objects of passion. For Euripides (and later for Seneca), Phaedra's love for Hippolytus is as much a perverison as her mother's mating with the bull. Tsvetaeva's Nurse, however, uses the reference to advance her argument. Tsvetaeva completely excises the idea of "unnatural" and incestuous passion (of which Phaedra was not really guilty, strictly speaking): her love is instead depicted as the longing of a young woman for a young man who can also fulfill her yearning for offspring.

The third scene opens with the Servant's story of Hippolyta's (Antiope's) battles and death. In the Servant's retelling, Hippolyta's death is a direct result of her love for her son (a theme crucial, it seems, for Tsvetaeva's interest in the legend). It is important for Tsvetaeva that Hippolyta died defending Athens from an attack by her own Amazons.[37] It is clear from Tsvetaeva's notes to the play that she was initially indecisive about whether to make Hippolytus's Amazon mother a happy wife of Theseus or his enemy. She settled on the latter and intended to use the fate of Hippolyta (Antiope) as the means to justify Hippolytus's own behavior in the play: "The image of Hippolyta as a woman who did not love her husband and who fought for her son is more valuable. Hippolyta, to the end, was entirely within the female kingdom. Theseus, to the end, was an enemy for her. Hippolyta did not love anyone except her son. Just the same ([concerning] relations with women) is Hippolytus."[38] Hippolyta, in the Servant's recollection, was caught in the conflict between her identity as a warrior and her duty as a mother, both roles emphasized by differences between her breasts — one severed ("*skudomjasaja*") and the other nourishing her child.[39]

Furthermore, the Servant's reminiscences of Antiope's selfless maternal love and sacrifice prompt Hippolytus to reflect sadly on his own childless state (doubts that were unknown to his Greek predecessor).[40] However, his wish for progeny does not neutralize his expressions of hatred for all womankind, which are akin to his ancient Euripidean counterpart's diatribe against women, in which he chastises them for being too talkative and oversexed. When the Nurse gives him a letter from Phaedra, Hippolytus throws down the tablet on which it is written, insulted by its clandestine nature. Shortly thereafter, Phaedra in a disjointed confession admits her passion for him, asking him to accept her love, not as a momentary whim, but as an eternal devotion. She even hints at the possibility of committing suicide together and finding union in death. Finally, curtly, he answers her plea for "A word! a single word only!": "Vermin!"[41]

It remains an open question whether Tsvetaeva was aware of the first version of Euripides' *Hippolytus* in which Phaedra makes her proposal of love directly to her stepson and which Euripides had to revise because the play outraged the audience by "the shamelessness of its Phaedra who openly declared her guilty passion to Hippolytus, and when rebuffed, just as brazenly confronted her husband face to face and herself accused Hippolytus of sexual assault."[42] If Tsvetaeva was aware of Euripides' early version of the play, she was clearly interested only in the first manifestation of Phaedra's unruly nature: her confession of love to Hippolytus. One of Tsvetaeva's main interests in both plays is the problem of feminine voice and speech.[43] While Tsvetaeva allows her Phaedra to speak, she at the same time seems to suggest "that despite its truth, feminine speech and writing are rejected or fatally misunderstood."[44] Hippolytus never reads the letter from Phaedra brought by the Nurse, and it is only in the end that that letter is read and understood by Theseus the way Phaedra intended it to be understood by Hippolytus. While Phaedra's letter in Euripides' *Hippolytus* is a weapon of deception and slander, in Tsvetaeva's play it is the baring of a loving heart. She takes Hippolytus's rejection and curse to her grave and, like Ariadne, without a word of reprimand.

Theseus does not blame the Nurse (who eventually confesses to her lies about Hippolytus in order to salvage Phaedra's honor) but rather the necessity of fate and Aphrodite's old hatred for him on account of his abandonment of Ariadne. Tsvetaeva thus reduces Phaedra's traditional guilt in Hippolytus's demise. In an unexpected final twist Theseus orders Hippolytus and Phaedra to be buried together under a myrtle tree in the unity of final unearthly love:

> *Tam, gde mirt shumit, eja stonom poln,*
> *Vozvedite im dvuedinyj kholm.*
> *Pust' khot' tam obov'et – mir bednym im!-*
> *Ippolitovu kost' – kost' Fedrina.*[45]

There, where the myrtle rustles, full of her groaning,

Raise to them a single doubled mound.
And so there let cover — peace to them, poor ones! —
Phaedra's bone — the bone of Hippolytus.

The semi-happy conclusion itself is borrowed from Schwab's version, aiming to provide some brightness in the generally hopeless situation. Tsvetaeva, however, turns Schwab's naïve and contrived optimism into an eternal union after death. One noteworthy detail of the final line is that "Phaedra's bone" ("*kost' Fedrina*") is the subject of the sentence whereas "Hippolytus's bone" ("*Ippolitovu kost'*") is the direct object. Thus even beyond the grave Phaedra remains the active agent of love and Hippolytus the recipient of her passion.[46] Furthermore, Tsvetaeva is also much more attentive to the details of Phaedra's death than Schwab, in that she selects the myrtle tree, sacred to Aphrodite, as Phaedra's chosen tool of suicide. Tsvetaeva herself explains that choice: "I would like to depict Phaedra as an incarnate myrtle, to twine her all around a myrtle sapling."[47] By choosing Aphrodite's tree, Phaedra insists on her right to passion and confirms it even in her final act.

The plot of *Phaedra* is more spare than that of *Ariadne*. It is also evident, as demonstrated above, that Tsvetaeva's dependence on Schwab's version of the story is rather doubtful, and that Euripides played a significant if not decisive role as her source for the structure of the plot, together probably with Seneca's *Phaedra* and Racine's *Phèdre*.[48] Seneca's *Phaedra* appears to have been a less influential source, although, as Thomson notes, it is the only play to begin (like Tsvetaeva's) with a series of extended choral hymns in praise of the hunt, followed by Phaedra's ill-conceived intrusion into the male world.[49]

The figure of the Nurse is especially remarkable in Tsvetaeva's divergence from her sources. Tsvetaeva's preliminary notes to the play show that she attached great importance to the role of the Nurse and defined it clearly:[50]

The role of the nurse? She is *not* a seductress…she only convinces Phaedra of her luck, gives her the last confidence…The role of the nurse is *very* important.

Thus Tsvetaeva viewed the Nurse as instrumental in Phaedra's demise only because the old woman wants to ensure the latter's happiness while fulfilling her own vicarious wishes. She enables the articulation and vocalization of Phaedra's sexuality and also makes it possible for Phaedra to replace Hippolytus as the tragic focus of the play. Phaedra's ability to voice her passion and pain is translated by Tsvetaeva into misunderstood and unfulfilled artistic potential.[51] Phaedra's failed love for Hippolytus translates into her failure in any self-expression, whether her own impossible maternity or her misread and misheard words.

Despite Tsvetaeva's self-proclaimed ignorance of the classics, this "modernized" version of Euripides' play is in some aspects more "classical" than any of its Russian predecessors. In her choice of Phaedra's method of death Tsvetaeva remains faithful to the ancient sources and turns away from Racine's suicide through poison back to Euripides' hanging, the exclusively feminine means of suicide in classical antiquity.[52] The play is also remarkable in following Aristotelian concepts of tragedy closely: the observation of the unity of time; the emphasis on the tragic flaw of the heroine brought down by a necessity beyond her control; the feelings of pity and fear – the two required conditions of the tragic *katharsis*. However, the most important aspect of Tsvetaeva's modifications of the traditional myth reflects her own position as a woman in juxtaposition with her male predecessors.[53] Antonina Gove rightly observes that a recurrent strain in the development of Tsvetaeva's lyric verse is "a rejection by the poet of the conventional roles imposed on the individual by society, particularly certain characteristics of the feminine role."[54] The outrageous (in the eyes of the Greek audience) element that forced Euripides to change the original plot of his *Hippolytus* becomes for Tsvetaeva the forbidden but inevitably chosen fruit: the emotional intensity of the female protagonist.

The real issue for Tsvetaeva, unlike Euripides, Seneca, or even Racine, is not Hippolytus's *hubris* in imagining that he, as a servant of the virgin goddess Artemis, could place himself above the powers of Aphrodite, the embodiment of sexual desire and femininity. Neither are any considerations of incest or inappropriate behavior on the part of Phaedra the moral focus of Tsvetaeva's drama. For Tsvetaeva the main concern in *Phaedra* is one of female sexuality and the right to articulate it.[55] In Euripides' play Phaedra's love is not only an inherited curse but also an *eros-nosos* (and eventually a cause of dishonorable behavior), as one of the choral odes explicitly states:

Love distills desire upon the eyes,
love brings bewitching grace into the heart
of those he would destroy.
I pray that love may never come to me
with murderous intent,
in rhythms measureless and wild. [56]

Although Tsvetaeva's Phaedra is still a victim of a mortal and uncontrollable disease, she is at the same time a sympathetic character whose love lacks the treachery and deceit of her ancient counterpart. Phaedra's only guilt is succumbing to and voicing her passion in a way that is socially inappropriate for a woman. Ariadne's silence in the first drama of the trilogy follows the expectations of the social norm: men woo or disparage and reject her and decide her fate. Phaedra is granted the self-affirmation denied to her sister. Although in *Ariadne* Theseus is as much the focus of the play as the title character, in *Phaedra* he is marginalized, while the female heroine is brought to the forefront.

Any interpretation of Tsvetaeva's poetry must move carefully between literature and biography. It is possible to assume that the circumstances of writing the classical plays (Tsvetaeva's expatriation and the loss of her native literary milieu) found reflection in Tsvetaeva's exploration of both the feminine voice and words in tragedy and the heroines' alienation from and rejection by their male counterparts. Although Tsvetaeva did not write explicitly about exile, the experience of it marked all the poetry she wrote abroad.[57] In *Phaedra* exile is metaphorically explored in Phaedra's sense of loneliness, isolation, and confusion.

Razminovenie: *Failed Relationships*

Most Greek tragic plots center on conflicts within in a family or house.[58] What makes the situation or crime presented in these ancient works tragically intolerable is not the crime itself (e.g., murder or adultery) but the relationship between perpetrator and victim. The horror is that Oedipus has slept with his mother, not that he has married the widow of the man he killed. Tsvetaeva also focuses on relationships in her tragedies, but in a slightly different fashion. For her it is the by-passed relationships which are intolerable: those which are denied, severed, failed, inadequate, or otherwise emptied of meaning. Looked at another way, while the traditional approach to tragedy seems to struggle with the unbearable closeness of families and spouses (e.g., Orestes strains to refuse to think of Clytemnestra as his mother), Tsvetaeva's characters strive for intimacy within these same relationships, and fail. *Razminovenie*[59] ("missed," "by-passed"[60]) is the Tsvetaevan term for such a failed relationship: it implies an intended but frustrated union. By examining the portrayal and construction of relationships and identities in *Ariadne* and *Phaedra*, one can begin to understand what constitutes the tragic in Tsvetaevan terms. While *Ariadne* and *Phaedra* do not portray relationships in the same fashion, both explore the problem of unbearable non-relationships. *Ariadne* robs relationships of meaning by presenting characters as doubles of each other, while *Phaedra* thwarts them by the fatality of inherited blood.

The net of relationships is constructed very curiously in *Ariadne* due to the pervasive doubling of characters.[61] It seems as though more than one character can claim a certain relationship which is usually understood as identifying only one person. For example, Theseus is named as son by Aegeus, Poseidon, and even Minos, who sees Theseus as a double of his dead son Androgeus. Since Theseus's paternity is questioned early on, the multiplicity of father figures effectively robs him of a father, because it is unclear who his father is. Theseus becomes fatherless through an excess of fathers.

Ariadne is doubled in Aphrodite (or she and Aphrodite double each other) in two ways.[62] First, the girl describes the goddess as her mistress, who speaks to her as a mother does to her child. This is a fairly straight-forward form of doubling: one expects children to resemble parents in looks, manner, or character. But Ariadne is Aphrodite's mouthpiece in the play, as well. In her first monologue she reports what Aphrodite has told her pupil about the ball of thread and the choosing of a husband; it is not always clear who is speaking, girl or goddess.[63] Later, she persuades Theseus to accept his sword and the thread by declaring herself the "mirror" of Aphrodite's will, a mere "messenger." Ariadne suggests by describing herself as a mirror that she is a human reflection of her goddess; as Aphrodite's messenger, she acts as a human proxy for the divine. Ariadne also reveals considerable (possibly divine) knowledge of the future when she foresees that Theseus will abandon her.

Ariadne is not the only character who doubles (or is doubled by) a divinity. Poseidon claims Theseus as a son because Theseus demonstrates a passion for justice. Theseus is doubled by Ariadne's other husband, Bacchus, the explicitly double-natured god.[64] The Minotaur, a double-natured monstrosity, is identified with Minos's power. The gift-giving, death-bearing sea is a pervasive sign of identity defined by doubleness. The two main characters themselves are double-natured: Ariadne is a figure of waking knowledge and sleeping ignorance, both present and absent; Theseus is sacrifice and conqueror, victim and betrayer. Yet the frequent images of the sea's foaming waves and the rock of the labyrinth, of Naxos, and of the fatal cliff, seem to suggest that there can be no confusion, no blurring, but only the violent, ever-changing, ever-constant contact of rock and wave.[65]

Almost all the characters are doubled by other characters,[66] and yet all the characters are quite isolated. One reason is that doubling may deny or question relationships while seeming to affirm them. For example, Theseus could be seen as a younger, fresher version of his father, Aegeus. But the inevitable comparison of the son to the father in the opening tableau invites the conclusion that the son is a noble, generous, brave hero, while the father is a weak, sly, unjust murderer. Another reason is that when multiple characters claim the same identity, that identity becomes less meaningful, as in the case of Theseus's multiple fathers.[67]

Each relationship presented in the play seems inadequate or repudiated. Ariadne divorces herself from her father's grief for an older brother she barely knew, and is rejected in turn by her father, because she is an unreliable girl. She helps Theseus slay her half-brother, thereby killing Minos's power. Theseus rejects Minos as a father figure and disobeys Aegeus. He abandons Ariadne and in grieving his loss, manages to precipitate Aegeus's death. So despite the veritable web of relationships that seem to exist, Minos is isolated in his grief, Ariadne is abandoned on Naxos, Aegeus kills himself in the belief that he is alone, and Theseus ends the play with neither father nor wife. Yet Theseus seeks to prove himself his father's son by his voyage to Crete and Ariadne tries to reach her father by banishing the ghost of Androgeus, and by pointing out that he has a loving daughter. However, both fathers interpret their children's actions as betrayals instead of attempts to affirm a bond. Later, Aegeus seems to forget his harsh words to Theseus, for he looks eagerly for the tell-tale sail. In his great desire to be united with his son, whom he believes dead, he then throws himself into the sea, effectively insuring that he and Theseus will never see each other alive. As a foil to the many rather confused relationships, the choruses (of youths and maidens to be sacrificed, and of Athenian citizens) sing first about relationships threatened (no spouses, no children for the victims; dead children for the citizens) and then saved. Ariadne's and Theseus's fatherlessness implies a certain rootlessness, a lack of a sense of belonging somewhere. Ariadne, in fact, leaves the human sphere completely; Theseus returns home but receives no homecoming.[68]

Phaedra seems to pursue further than *Ariadne* the intolerability of non-relationships, and how they come about (or how relationships do not come about, are by-passed). The first tableau begins with a long paean by the chorus of youths (Hippolytus's companions) to the goddess Artemis. They also assert their childlessness, a natural result of chastity. But it is not only women who are set aside by the young hunters. They have chosen to live isolated in the forest, cut off not only from sexuality, but family, the larger community, and personal history. Along with the role of husband, they reject the role of father, and thus become unnatural children.[69]

When Phaedra stumbles into the campsite, she and Hippolytus identify themselves to each other, not by name (that is, where they fit in the mortal scheme of relationships) but by the goddesses each serves – Hippolytus Artemis, Phaedra Aphrodite. Names are not exchanged at this point, as if the two resist being identified as being someone's wife, son, daughter, or sister.

When the Nurse tries to coax from Phaedra the source of the queen's illness, she reminds her nursling of the strength of their relationship, and exhorts Phaedra to speak by claiming that there are two fatal voices in one's life: the voice of blood, which is the voice of one's mother, and the voice of milk, which is the voice of one's nurse, one's second mother. In fact, the Nurse will argue that Phaedra's love for Hippolytus is not incestuous, because the queen is merely Hippolytus's stepmother, not his blood-mother.[70] When Phaedra finally confesses her love for Hippolytus, the Nurse sees no guilt, but considers the unnatural relationship to be Phaedra's marriage and faithfulness to Theseus: Phaedra has not been made a mother by her husband of ten years. The Nurse insists that without a child, Phaedra's marriage to Theseus is nothing but lechery. Unlike in *Ariadne*, in this play we see a relationship between two women, although the focus of Phaedra is Hippolytus, while the Nurse's focus is Phaedra.[71]

In the third tableau, the Servant describes to Hippolytus the death of Antiope, telling how she fought in defense of Athens against her own tribe, the Amazons, and emphasizing that she fought for her son. Antiope was willing to turn her back on her old family to ensure the survival of the new. Hippolytus feels keenly the irony of her sacrifice, since he will never have children. His dead mother is known to him only indirectly, through stories and dreams, his children will never be, and in the confrontation that follows between Hippolytus and Phaedra yet another impossible, failed relationship is played out.

Phaedra hangs herself, not in the traditional, wifely way,[72] but outside, from a myrtle, with her belt. By choosing not to hang herself in their bedroom, but from the bough of a tree, she denies her identity as Theseus's wife. Because Hippolytus is frequently associated with forest and thicket, Phaedra is asserting her relationship to Hippolytus (as a rejected lover, but nonetheless, it is her failed connection to him, and not to Theseus, that is the immediate reason for her death). Her corpse is the fruit of neglected (by Theseus) and rejected (by Hippolytus) love — love wasted, "by-passed."

The only blood-relationship of the play is that of Theseus and Hippolytus. Ironically, this is the weakest bond in the work.[73] Hippolytus and Theseus are never on stage together until the hunter's dead body is carried in. Hippolytus refers to himself as Antiope's son more frequently than as the son of Theseus. Theseus, having heard the false evidence of the Nurse, invokes Poseidon's curse and so destroys his son. Hippolytus seems much closer to his dead mother: he worships and emulates the chaste huntress Artemis, is troubled by his mother's warning in a dream, and is fascinated by Antiope's prowess in battle and brave death. But Hippolytus fails her, because he is childless, and so ends the life that she died to preserve.

Razminovenie, the "by-passed" relationship, is a crucial aspect to the Tsvetaevan concept of tragedy. The point is not that characters are isolated or dead at the end of a play (which is hardly remarkable in tragedy) but how they are isolated, namely by the failure or inadequacy of their human relationships. It is not that Hippolytus is Phaedra's stepson that makes life unbearable for her, it is that he is not her lover. The problem is not that Theseus is her husband, but that he, in a fundamental way, is not her husband. In *Ariadne* the longed-for union of Aegeus and

Theseus is in part frustrated by the king's too-great love. The incompletion of the father-son union is directly linked to the broken bond of Ariadne and Theseus: due to his grief at leaving Ariadne, Theseus forgets to change the sail. Because Theseus loves Ariadne so much, he cedes her to Bacchus. At the end of *Ariadne* all the father-figures are absent: Minos distant and powerless, Aegeus dead, Poseidon silent. *Phaedra*, on the other hand, underlines the barrenness of its characters by pointing that each represents the end of a family line: Phaedra, Hippolytus, the Nurse are all childless, and Theseus joins them.

Sisterly Plays: Imagery and Structure

The plays are bound not only by thematic concerns, but by images and words that are repeated and layered in meaning as they appear in new contexts. Tsvetaeva's masterful use of imagery, which forms a web of associations, recalls Peter Burian's description of the language of Aeschylus in the *Oresteia*: "he…invents new words and startling periphrases, tests the limits of Greek syntax, and plays brilliantly with ambiguity and enigma…"[74] While the language of Tsvetaeva's tragedies is not quite as dense or as multiply charged as that of the *Oresteia*, nevertheless, she, too, uses "associative repetition"[75] to suggest relationships between the two plays and among characters and situations.

A word such as *glyba* ("stone block") shows how the significance of a single word can be enriched and resonate with added meaning. In *Ariadne*, when Ariadne is waiting anxiously outside the labyrinth, she says, "*Glyb verolomna tish'…Glyb nemoty – ne mene / Chuvstv nenadezhen vopl'.* (The silence of the stone blocks is treacherous…The scream of my feelings / Is as unreliable as the muteness of these stone blocks)."[76] She is lamenting the dreadful silence of the labyrinth. Then, hearing a loud thud, she exclaims, "*Ne – glyba – osela!* (This is not a block tumbling)."[77] Now the block is no longer a sign of silence, but of a significant yet uninterpretable sound – something great has fallen, but is it the Minotaur or Theseus? Its ominous significance deepens as it becomes more fully metaphorical: later, when Ariadne is resisting Theseus's demands that she come away with him, she says, "*Zane: kak glyba / Strast' moja! Zane: na gibel' / Strast' moja tebe!* (For like a stone / Is my passion! For my passion / Is your ruin!)."[78] And indeed her choice of Theseus as husband, thereby binding him to Aphrodite through her actions as well as by his oaths, proves to be disastrous for the hero. The word is next seen in *Phaedra*, again associated with a pitiless goddess, but now it is Artemis who is praised by the Hippolytus's chorus of friends: "*Golye glyby – tserdtse eja!* (Bare rock-blocks her heart!)"[79] The ominous stone blocks that in *Ariadne* are obstacles (the labyrinth) or a heavy burden (ruinous passion) become, in the context of the chorus, laudable defenses against the muck of *eros*. Yet these defenses are not perfect for those who do not worship Artemis. When Phaedra finally makes her stumbling confession to Hippolytus, the stone block appears again: "*...nachalom stuk byl / Serdtsa, do kusta, do roga, / Do vsego — stuk, tochno boga / Vstretila, stuk, tochno glybu... / — Sdvinula! — nachalom ty byl...* (...the beginning was the beat / Of a heart, *before* the bush, *before* the horn, / Before everything — a beat, just as if I had met / A god, a beat, just as if a block of stone... / — I had moved! — the beginning was you...)."[80] The block (which metaphorically marks the onset of Phaedra's passion as well as Phaedra's now broken silence) has been shoved aside, and Phaedra's fatal language spills freely. The ruinous associations from *Ariadne* are again evoked, adding to and resonating with the layered meanings: maze, obstacle, silence, ruin, portentous sound, the freedom to speak of desire. The last time the word is used, it is spoken by Theseus as he curses his son to death: "*Pod ego stopoj / Zemlju vskolybni! / Glyboj poperek! / Svoroj po pjatam / Pashchenkovym...* (Under his foot / Shake the earth! / Like a stone block across! / Like a pack of hounds on the heels / Of a suckling...)."[81] As Theseus calls down his curse and imagines its fulfillment, he uses an image already associated with disaster, ruin, and the pitilessness of the gods. Here the stone block is desired as an obstacle to bring death more swiftly to his son, whom he imagines as hunted prey. Yet of course the curse will be revealed to be another ramification of decisions made in the shadow of the labyrinth's stones.[82]

    Even an instance of a word picked up from a scant two lines in *Ariadne* and used once in *Phaedra* can be striking. Bacchus reminds Theseus that all he has to offer Ariadne is the maggot (*cherv'*), death; in the second play's *agōn*, between Phaedra and the Nurse, Phaedra cries out that the Nurse, with her persistent questioning, is like a gnawing worm (*cherv'*). The word is used at the crisis point in both scenes: it is the thought that he could spare Ariadne the decay of mortality that turns Theseus to abandoning her; it is the Nurse's relentless, cunning persistence that extracts the secret of her love from Phaedra.

There are also sets of images that are developed (a boat taking on a wave; allusions to and representations of delirious speech; the Cretan labyrinth that becomes the thickets of Troezen). The colors black and white, so obviously and literally important in *Ariadne* as the significant sails of Theseus's returning ship, link the plays on several levels. Aegeus broods on the colors at length; the chorus of citizens grieves when it sees the sail, repeatedly naming the colors. When Theseus explains the ghastly error, the chorus of youths explains the black sails by a deepening of the association of black with death and despair: to the grieving eye, only the color black is bearable. In *Phaedra*, immediately before Theseus's second joyless homecoming, the Nurse swears to make white seem black and black seem white by lying to the king. The Nurse and Theseus continually insist that if Hippolytus is black, then Phaedra is white, and vice versa. The two homecomings are linked, because these two colors (proverbially so distinct, allowing no confusion) are misleading, and their confusion brings about Theseus's father's death on the one hand (from the hero's grief at the loss of Ariadne) and his son's death on the other (from his anger at the loss of Phaedra).

Similarities of structure also link the two plays. Each begins with a stranger intruding and setting off events: *Ariadne* with the Foreigner (Poseidon) in Athens, stirring up the populace and instigating the departure of Theseus on the tribute ship, *Phaedra* with the less purposeful foreigner, Phaedra, stumbling upon the encampment of Hippolytus and his friends, an encounter that will also have disastrous consequences. The two unhappy homecomings of Theseus are described in similar terms. For example, in *Ariadne* Theseus is offended by the Athenians' silent reception and complains that his father has not come to meet him (when ironically, his father went to meet him by flinging himself in the sea). In *Phaedra*, Theseus repeats both the joyless homecoming he experienced in *Ariadne* (the palace is deserted and silent) and the lack of a proper fatherly welcome (he is rebuked by the chorus of Hippolytus's friends for not meeting his son's corpse as a father should). In both plays there is the similar (but not identical) scene of a father not waiting for full news of his son before he takes irrevocable and tragic action (Aegeus's suicide and Theseus's curse). The choruses in the two plays are also distinctive elements that underline the relationship between the two works. Although usually they lyrically express grief or praise, they can be more active. For example, the Chorus of Citizens in the first tableau of *Ariadne* and the Chorus of Youths in the final tableau of *Phaedra* both confront the king (Aegeus, Theseus) with his injustice.

Ariadne and Phaedra, so different in some ways, are both prophetic speakers. Ariadne speaks of the impossibility of her and Theseus's love, specifically pointing to the not-always-benevolent attention of Aphrodite and the possibility of Theseus having a god as a rival. Phaedra in her delirium speaks repeatedly of the sound of a horse's galloping and of a fateful myrtle branch bearing fruit (anguish), thereby predicting both her own and Hippolytus's deaths. Both the sisters are last seen and spoken of as sleepers: Ariadne who is indeed sleeping, and Phaedra who is dead. Hippolytus joins the women: three sleepers whose bodies and fates the hero Theseus ultimately interprets and decides, while they lie silent.

For reasons that remain unknown, *Helen*, the last play of the intended trilogy, was never written. It is possible that for Tsvetaeva *Phaedra* represented the pinnacle of experimentation with classical drama and thus, after writing it, she abandoned the form altogether.[83] It is also possible that the lack of support and critical acclaim for her tragedies led Tsvetaeva, motivated by more practical considerations, to take a new direction in her poetry that would enable her to fare better with the critics and publishing venues.

In this context, it may be helpful also to make a few remarks about the diction of both poems. While *Ariadne* is stylistically uniform and easier to read, *Phaedra* appears more innovative in its use of Russian folk songs, neologisms, and archaisms, as if the play were clinging to the core and fabric of the lost mother tongue. In that respect both plays stand in a contradictory relation to at least one of Tsvetaeva's Russian predecessors in neo-classical tragedy: Tsvetaeva's diction is far removed from Ivanov's high-flown and at times difficult language and allusions, which require intricate knowledge of Greek mythology and literature. Tsvetaeva's plays, where the conventional language is pushed to its limits, are still far more touching pieces of poetry and are replete with emotions familiar to a reader of Tsvetaeva's lyric poetry. In these plays Tsvetaeva shines with full force as an innovator of Russian poetic language: she omits verbs, uses difficult phrases allowed only by the inflected language, and clothes dramatic action in an equally intensely dramatic rhythm of verse. A feeling of despair haunts her experimentation with the language of this play, despair familiar to a poet physically removed from the space that resounds with her native tongue, the space she tries to recreate in her poetry.

It is perhaps because of the difficult diction of both plays, but especially of *Phaedra*, that they did not win Tsvetaeva any acclaim. Tsvetaeva's classical plays have not been treated kindly by either contemporary or later critics of her poetry.[84] Tomas Venclova went so far as to call *Phaedra* a "chaotic and anarchic work."[85] There is no doubt that even for a native speaker of Russian these plays present a difficult reading challenge with their tangle of language, unusual meter, and often inexplicable choice of words.

Furthermore, the difficulty of staging Tsvetaeva's plays becomes especially apparent in her choice of diction for them. Tsvetaeva remained unwavering in her rejection of theater as a medium for her dramas. In this respect her neo-classical attempts were akin (perhaps unintentionally so) to those of Ivanov and Annensky. The plays need to be read, not performed, because they represent for Tsvetaeva first and foremost a form of literature that must remain static for the reader and faithful to its literary sources and thus resists the interpretation inherent in any staged performance. The supreme importance of the word, both spoken and written, penetrates the plot as well as the meaning of the play. Unlike Annensky's tragedies, the plays do not provide even stage directions or descriptions of the appearances of the characters.[86] All of the specifics are left to the imagination of the reader.

In one of her earliest poems (written in 1913), "*Moim stikham napisannym tak rano ...*"[87] ("To my poems written so early..."), Tsvetaeva expresses doubt about her poetic legacy and hopes that time would prove their quality. The poem ends with an optimistic exclamation:

> *Moim stikham, kak dragotsennym vinam,*
> *Nastanet svoj chered.*
> For my poems, as for precious wines
> Their turn will come ...

It seems that Tsvetaeva's classical plays have finally entered that stage of increasing, and much deserved, interest. What were perceived at first as their shortcomings (unusual diction, entangled verbal texture, idiosyncratic use of well-known myths) can now be seen as yet another proof of Tsvetaeva's innovative and progressive poetic vision that left an indelible impression on Russian poetic language.

NOTES

[1] Ivanov was a poet, critic, translator, and scholar. He wrote two tragedies on classical subjects, *Tantalus* (1905) and *Prometheus* (published 1919), and translated Aeschylus's *The Suppliant Women*, *The Persians*, *Seven against Thebes*, and the *Oresteia* trilogy. Annensky was a playwright, poet, literary critic, and translator of Euripides (his translations of all Euripides' plays were published between 1907 and 1921). Annensky also wrote original tragedies on classical subjects: *Melanippa the Philosopher* (1901), *King Ixion* (1902), *Laodamia* (1906), and *Thamyrus Cythraoede* (1913).

[2] See the letter to Yury Ivask dated April 4, 1933, in Marina Tsvetaeva, *Stikhotvorenija i poemy v pjati tomakh* [Lyric poetry and narrative poems in five volumes], ed. Alexander Sumerkin (New York: Russica Publishers, 1980-90), 5: 469.

[3] Anastasija Tsvetaeva, *Vospominanija*, 1st ed. (Moscow: Sovetskij pisatel', 1971), 23. For a more detailed account of Ivan Tsvetaev's academic career see E. D. Frolov, *Russkaja nauka ob antichnosti: istoriografiicheskie ocherki* [Russian studies of antiquity: Historigraphical notes] (St. Petersburg: Izdatel'stvo S. Peterburgskogo universiteta, 1999), 202-4.

[4] Alexander Bakhrakh, ed. *Pis'ma Mariny Tsvetaevoj* [Letters of Marina Tsvetaeva], *Mosty* 5 (1960): 299-318; *Mosty* 6 (1961): 322 and 337.

[5] Cited in Tomas Venclova, "On Russian Mythological Tragedy: Vjačeslav Ivanov and Marina Cvetaeva," in *Myth in Literature*, ed. A. Kodjak, K. Pomorska, and S. Rudy (Columbus, OH: Slavica Publishers, 1985), 108, letter dated April 4, 1933.

[6] See Serena Vitale, ed. and trans. *Marina Cvetaeva: Deserti luoghi: Lettere 1925-1941* [Marina Tsvetaeva: Desert places: Letters 1925-1941] (Milan: Adelphi Edizioni, 1989), 172.

[7] See Venclova, 100, and Simon Karlinsky, *Marina Tsvetaeva: The Woman, Her World, and Her Poetry* (Cambridge: Cambridge University Press, 1986), 181-82. Tsvetaeva cited Schwab as her source in the letter to Yury Ivask dated April 4, 1933. In the same letter she added: "I was never under anyone's influence. I began with writing, not with reading poets." Another source identified by Tsvetaeva herself was Heinrich Stoll's *Die Sagen der klassischen Altertums* (1862). See Tsvetaeva's letter to Rainer Maria Rilke of 22 August 1926 in Marina Tsvetaeva, *Sobranie sochinenii v semi tomakh* [Collected works in seven volumes], ed. Anna Saakjants and Lev Mnukhin (Moscow: Ellis Lak, 1994-95), 7: 73. The letter may be found in English in *Letters Summer 1926* by Boris Pasternak, Marina Tsvetayeva, and Rainer Maria Rilke (San Diego: Harcourt Brace Jovanovich, 1985).

[8] Michael Makin, *Marina Tsvetaeva: The Poetics of Appropriation* (Oxford: Clarendon Press, 1993), 268.

[9] See Hanna Ruutu, *Patterns of Transcendence – Classical Myth in Marina Tsvetaeva's Poetry of the 1920s* (Helsinki: University of Helsinki, 2006), 14. See also Maria Razumovskaja, *Marina Tsvetaeva: Mif' i dejstvitel'nost'* (London: Overseas Publications Interchange, 1983), 67. Translated by Aleksey Gibson as *Marina Tsvetaeva: A Critical Biography* by Maria Razumovsky (Newcastle-upon-Tyne, UK: Bloodaxe Books, 1994).

[10] *Sobranie sochinenii* 4: 545. Tsvetaeva's adherence to German literature also stemmed from her mother's heritage. Her mother Maria Alexandrovna Mein (1868-1906) was the half-Polish daughter of a wealthy Baltic German businessman and publisher, A. D. Mein. See Karlinsky, 3.

[11] See Ruutu, 14.

[12] Venclova, 102.

[13] Marina Tsvetaeva, *Teatr* [Theater], ed. A. Efron and A. Saakjants. (Moscow: Iskusstvo, 1988), 342.

[14] *Teatr*, 360.

[15] See Sumerkin's commentary in *Stikhotvorenija i poemy*, 5: 469. He notes that Tsvetaeva decided to change the title for the trilogy in October 1924.

[16] Marina Tsvetaeva, *Pis'ma k A. Teskovoj* (Prague: Academia, 1969), 56. In her notes on *Phaedra* she writes: "Phaedra is thought of by me as *of the bone – not* of the flesh. The flesh is Helen." *Teatr*, 379.

[17] Venclova, 89.

[18] See Rebecca Armstrong, *Cretan Women: Pasiphae, Ariadne, and Phaedra in Latin Poetry* (Oxford: Oxford University Press, 2006), 12.

[19] The play was originally called *Theseus* but later renamed *Ariadne* to avoid confusion with the whole trilogy. It was completed in 1924 and published in 1927.

[20] Rose Lafoy duly notes that Ariadne has often been considered an embodiment of Aphrodite, which also explains her reliance on and connection to Aphrodite as her mother figure and her protectress in the play. Rose Lafoy, ed. and trans., Ariane: *Tragédie de Marina Cvetaeva* [Ariadne: A tragedy by Marina Tsvetaeva] (Clermont-Ferrand: Faculté des Lettres et Sciences Humaines de l'Université de Clerment-Ferrand, 1981), 112.

[21] The story of Theseus and Ariadne appears in many ancient sources starting with Homer's *Odyssey* and ending with Ovid's *Heroides* and *Metamorphoses*. For a detailed account of them see Lafoy and Armstrong. The most famous recounting of Ariadne's abandonment is Catullus 64. 52-75 where the *ecphrasis* [descriptive picture] on the coverlet for the marriage bed of Peleus and Thetis depicts Ariadne engulfed in rage and grief, cursing Theseus as she watches his sail disappearing at sea. In *Heroides* 10 Ovid transforms Ariadne's indignant speech in Catullus's *ecphrasis* into a letter. Although Ovid's *Heroides*

might have been one of the sources for Ariadne's lament by Tsvetaeva, Ovid had also written it with Catullus in mind. See Armstrong, 222.

[22] Diodorus Siculus, *The Library of History*, 4. 61. 5; 5. 51.4.

[23] Tsvetaeva also intended originally to use fear of the god as the reason for Theseus's betrayal, but then changed her mind, according to Makin, 277, under the influence of the end of her love affair with Konstantin Rodzevich.

[24] Marina Tsvetaeva, *Neizdannoe: Svodnye tetradi* [Unpublished works: Collected notebooks], ed. E.B. Korkina and I. D. Shevelenko (Moscow: Ellis Lak, 1997), 265.

[25] *Neizdannoe: Svodnye tetradi*, 299. See Ruutu, 112, for a more detailed discussion of Tsvetaeva's notes to the play.

[26] Or "intentionally dishonouring behavior," according to the *Oxford Classical Dictionary*, 3rd ed., s.v. "Hubris."

[27] It is only in the lyric cycle *Ariadne*, written in 1923 (before the play was finished) and included in her 1928 collection *After Russia* (*Posle Rossii*), that Ariadne receives the right of final complaint so conspicuously missing in the play. In the tragedy, however, Tsvetaeva deprives Ariadne of the Catullan rage, despair, and curses originally granted to the heroine of her lyric cycle.

[28] *Stikhotvorenija i poemy*, 5: 241. See Sibelan Forrester, "Daphne's Tremor: Tsvetaeva and the Feminine in Classical Myth and Statuary," *Indiana Slavic Studies* 11 (2000): 367.

[29] *Stikhotvorenija i poemy*, 5: 243.

[30] Tsvetaeva's emphasis.

[31] Euripides, *Alcestis; The Medea; The Heracleidae; Hippolytus*, ed. David Grene and Richmond Lattimore (Chicago: The University of Chicago Press, 1955), 172.

[32] For the importance of the figure of the Amazon in Tsvetaeva's poetics see Forrester; Antonina F. Gove, "The Feminine Stereotype and Beyond: Role Conflict and Resolution in the Poetics of Marina Tsvetaeva," *Slavic Review* 36.2 (1977): 247; and Pamela Perkins and Albert Spaulding Cook, *The Burden of Sufferance: Women Poets of Russia* (New York and London: Garland Publishing, 1993), 19, n. 2.

[33] Euripides, 165-66, 189-190. There is little doubt that Tsvetaeva was aware of this Euripidean tragedy. Annensky, Zelinsky, and Merezhkovsky had all translated *Hippolytus*. These translations appeared between 1902 and 1920, and several of the editions included commentaries.

[34] Euripides, 190.

[35] *Stikhotvorenija i poemy*, 5: 284-85.

[36] Euripides, 177.

[37] Makin, 285.

[38] Cited and translated by Makin, 285.

[39] *Stikhotvorenija i poemy*, 5: 294.

[40] *Stikhotvorenija i poemy*, 5: 294.

[41] *Stikhotvorenija i poemy*, 5: 300.

[42] Froma Zeitlin, "The Power of Aphrodite: Eros and the Boundaries of the Self in the *Hippolytus*," in *Directions in Euripidean Criticism: A Collection of Essays*, ed. Peter Burian (Durham, NC: Duke University Press, 1985), 52. See also David Grene's introduction to *Hippolytus* in Euripides, 158.

[43] Fox, Maria Stadter, *The Troubling Play of Gender: The Phaedra Dramas of Tsvetaeva, Yourcenar, and H.D.* (Selinsgrove, PA: Susquehanna University Press, 2001), 40.

[44] Fox, 40.

[45] *Stikhotvorenija i poemy*, 5: 315.

[46] In an earlier draft, the Nurse in her final words requests the bodies be laid together under the myrtle, "where they never lay." *Teatr*, 377.

[47] Cited in Venclova, 106.

[48] The latter is more likely to have been on Tsvetaeva's mind since Tsvetaeva idolized Sarah Bernhardt all her life and could not possibly have remained ignorant of her most celebrated role. It has been noted, however, that Racine's play makes no use of a chorus and Tsvetaeva's *Phaedra* reveals no traces of the academic style characteristic of French Classicists. See R. D. B. Thomson, "Tsvetaeva's Play *Fedra*: An Interpretation," *Slavic and East European Journal* 6.3 (1989): 343; Ruutu, 13; and Lafoy, 193. For a detailed analysis of Tsvetaeva's *Phaedra* in the context of Baroque drama, see N. O. Osipova, *Tvorchestvo M. I. Tsvetaevoj v kontekste kul'turnoj mifologii serebrianogo veka* [The work of M. I. Tsvetaeva in the context of the cultural mythology of the Silver Age] (Kirov: Izdatale'stvo VGPU, 2000). Tsvetaeva also would have known two of Osip Mandelshtam's poems: one is the short poem of 1914 on Anna Akhmatova ("*Vpoloborota, o pechal'*" -- "Half turning around, O sadness") in which she is compared with Racine's *Phèdre* in Rachel's (Élisa Félix's) famous rendition; another is "*Ja ne uvizhu znamenitoj Fedry ...*" ("I will not see the famous Phaedra...") written in 1915, which refers specifically to Racine's play. Another poem by Mandelshtam about Phaedra, which opens the poet's collection *Tristia*, was written in 1916 and draws on *Phèdre* and *Hippolytus* alike. See Gregory Freidin, *A Coat of Many Colors: Osip Mandelshtam and His Mythologies of Self-Presentation* (Berkeley: University of California Press, 1987), 91-99, and Clarence Brown, *Mandelshtam* (Cambridge: Cambridge University Press, 1973), 207-52.

[49] Thomson, 343.

[50] Marina Tsvetaeva, *Neizdannoe: Zapisnye knizhki v dvukh tomakh* [Unpublished works: Notebooks in two volumes], vol. 2: 1919-1939, ed. E.B. Korkina, M.G. Krutikova (Moscow: Ellis Lak, 2001), 305. All the emphases are Tsvetaeva's.

[51] For Tsvetaeva's play on the words "sounds" ("*zvuki*") and "letters" ("*bukvy*") as the building block of her depiction of Phaedra as a poet, see Thomson, 346-347. See also Svetlana Boym, *Death in Quotation Marks: Cultural*

Myths of the Modern Poet (Cambridge, MA: Harvard University Press, 1991), 234.

[52] Eve Cantarella, "Dangling Virgins: Myth, Ritual, and the Place of Women in Ancient Greece" in *The Female Body in Western Culture: Contemporary Perspectives*, ed. Susan R. Suleiman (Cambridge, MA: Harvard University Press, 1986), 57-67.

[53] On women in Russian literature and the Russian cultural tradition see Barbara Heldt, *Terrible Perfection: Women and Russian Literature* (Bloomington: Indiana University Press, 1987).

[54] Gove, 231. For the theoretical basis of the perception of "female poetry" ("*zhenskaja poezija*") in opposition to "ladies' poetry" ("*damskaja poezija*") see I. D. Shevelenko, *Literaturnyj put' Tsvetaevoj: Ideologija-poetika-identichnost' avtora v kontekste epokhi* [The literary journey of Tsvetaeva: The ideology-poetics-identity of the author in the context of her time] (Moscow: Novoe Literaturnoe Obozrenie, 2002), 64-74; and Perkins and Cook, 1-22, esp. 14-17, who point out (2) that the complexities of the lives and poetry of women poets in Russia "challenge Western feminist criticism."

[55] See Thomson, 343. For a more recent discussion of Tsvetaeva's sympathetic portrayal of a powerful femininity see Alyssa W. Dinega, *A Russian Psyche: The Poetic Mind of Marina Tsvetaeva* (Madison: University of Wisconsin Press, 2001).

[56] Euripides, 185. Compare the Nurse in the final tableau of Tsvetaeva's *Phaedra*: "Whom the gods destroy − / − Eh! − they deprive of reason!" *Stikhotvorenija i poemy*, 5: 302.

[57] Ute Stock, "Marina Tsvetaeva: The Concrete and Metaphoric Discourse of Exile," *The Modern Language Review* 96.3 (July 2001): 776.

[58] It is true that there are some that do not. *Prometheus Bound, Philoctetes,* and *Hecuba* spring to mind.

[59] Kroth provides a useful and thorough examination of the concept of *razminovenie*, and suggests possible translations range from "parting ways" to "transcendence." Anya M. Kroth, "Dichotomy and *Razminovenie* in the Work of Marina Cvetaeva," PhD diss., University of Michigan, 1977. See her first chapter, especially pp. 7-10.

[60] These English versions of *razminovenie* are taken from Ronald Hingley's very brief discussion of the two plays in his *Nightingale Fever: Russian Poets in Revolution* (New York: Knopf, 1981), 150-152.

[61] Tsvetaeva had thought about the double-nature of *Ariadne*'s characters in early notes on the play. *Teatr*, 371-372.

[62] "Doubling" is an awkward way of describing the Ariadne/Aphrodite relationship. More accurate might be to say that Ariadne is double-natured: on the one hand, a maiden princess, on the other, the goddess of love. In her notes, Tsvetaeva considers Aphrodite and Bacchus as a pair, adding to the confusion of girl and goddess. *Teatr*, 372.

[63]Lafoy, 112-113.

[64]Lafoy suggests that the off-stage voice may be "tout simplement, la voix de la tentation qui existe en chacun d'entre nous: celle de l'ambition (devenir un Dieu!), celle des désirs secrets, celle de la lâcheté – cette voix toujours capable de se découvrir de bonnes raisons et d'apaiser la conscience par sophismes [quite simply, the voice of temptation which exists in each one of us: that of ambition (to become a God!), that of secret desires, that of cowardice—that voice which is always capable of discovering good reasons and of appeasing the conscience by sophistries]." Lafoy, 153. It is an interesting notion, but unlikely. Tsvetaeva is generally not a fan of moral cowards (though she is of lost causes), and it is characteristic for her to narrate a love destroyed by excess of love.

[65]Kroth sees the antitheses (e.g. rock v. wave) of Tsvetaeva's poetic world not as dual (that is, two separate) entities, but as dichotomous (paired). Anya M. Kroth, "Androgyny as an Exemplary Feature of Marina Tsvetaeva's Dichotomous Poetic Vision," *Slavic Review*, 38 (1979): 563-582.

[66]Lafoy, 113, mentions the doubled pairs Theseus/Androgeus and Aegeus/Minos, and remarks that "entre les êtres il n'est pas de frontières très nettes, que chacun est à la fois multiple et morcelé [between beings there are no clear boundaries, each one is both multiple and fractured]."

[67]Again, "doubling" may not be the most felicitous term. While Theseus has multiple doubles, these doubles do not necessarily double each other (e.g., Bacchus is not a double of Aegeus). It is as if Theseus finds a different mirror wherever he looks: each image is his double, and together they produce a multiplicity of Theseuses.

[68]Efron and Saakjants cite Tsvetaeva's comment that "Theseus is cursed by Aphrodite and must, one after another, lose all whom he loves." *Teatr*, 371.

[69]Hippolytus will describe himself as his parents' tomb. The youths also disdain fatherhood because "To multiply is to divide oneself!" *Stikhotvorenija i poemy*, 5: 268. In dismissing Hippolytus's dream of Antiope, the band will proclaim, "What is not us – / Is mirage." *Stikhotvorenija i poemy*, 5: 274. The youths happily embrace a splendid, sterile self-centeredness.

[70]Tsvetaeva wrote quite a bit about her own mother and her own experience of motherhood. See, for example, her prose work, "*Mat' i muzyka*," in Marina Tsvetaeva, *Izbrannaja proza v dvukh tomakh, 1917-1937* [Selected prose in two volumes, 1917-1937], ed. Alexander Sumerkin (New York: Russica Publishers, 1979), 172-190; translated by J. M. King as "Mother and Music" in *A Captive Spirit: Selected Prose of Marina Tsvetaeva*, ed. J.M. King (Ann Arbor, MI: Ardis, 1980). Laura Weeks discusses mothers and daughters in Tsvetaeva's life and art, focusing particularly on the Greek idea of *kore* and the Demeter-Persephone myth, in "'I Named Her Ariadna...': The Demeter-Persephone Myth in Tsvetaeva's Poems for Her Daughter," *Slavic Review*, 49 (Winter 1990): 568-584.

[71]See Marina Tsvetaeva [Cvetaeva], "Lettera all'Amazzone" in *Le notti fiorentini, Lettera all'Amazzone*, ed. Serena Vitale (Milan: Mondadori, 1983). The letter is in French (with an Italian translation). Addressing Natalie Clifford Barney (1876-1972), Tsvetaeva affirms that love between two women is the best love, but doomed to rupture, because sooner or later the younger woman is going to want a child, and leave the older woman for a man.

[72]See Nicole Loraux's excellent and too short work *Tragic Ways of Killing a Woman* (Cambridge: Harvard University Press, 1987) for a good look at the way virgins and wives die in Greek tragedy.

[73]Tsvetaeva identifies the blood-relationship as the maternal relationship almost exclusively. Paternity seems much less elemental and more superficial or even mobile. See the discussion of *Ariadne* above. Tsvetaeva appears to consider fatherhood a very fluid bond. On this point it might be interesting to examine how Tsvetaeva attributes fathers (poetic and otherwise) to her son Mur, according to Jane Taubman's book, *A Life Through Poetry: Marina Tsvetaeva's Lyric Diary* (Columbus, OH: Slavica, 1989).

[74] Peter Burian, introduction to *The Oresteia* by Aeschylus, trans. Alan Shapiro and Peter Burian (Oxford and New York: Oxford University Press), 28.

[75] Burian borrows this term from Anne Lebeck. Burian, 29, 37.

[76] *Stikhotvorenija i poemy*, 5: 234.

[77] *Stikhotvorenija i poemy*, 5: 235.

[78] *Stikhotvorenija i poemy*, 5: 240.

[79] *Stikhotvorenija i poemy*, 5: 270.

[80] *Stikhotvorenija i poemy*, 5: 299.

[81] *Stikhotvorenija i poemy*, 5: 306.

[82] Another related constellation of meaning in the plays clusters around the word *kamen'*, "stone." In this essay the richness of Tsvetaeva's language is indicated only, not explored in depth.

[83] Makin, 294.

[84] See Karlinsky, 184.

[85] Venclova, 104.

[86] On differences between Annensky's tragedies and Tsvetaeva's *Ariadne*, see Andrew Kahn, "Chorus and Monologue in Marina Tsvetaeva's *Ariadna*: An Analysis of Their Structure, Versification and Themes," in *Marina Tsvetaeva: One Hundred Years; Papers from the Tsvetaeva Centenary Symposium, Amherst College, MA, 1992*, ed. Viktoria Schweitzer et al., 162-93, Modern Russian Literature and Culture 32 (Oakland, CA: Berkeley Slavic Specialities, 1994).

[87] *Stikhotvorenija i poemy*, 1: 140.

ARIADNE

Theseus abandoning Ariadne. Apulian Red Figure stamnos, ca 400 -390 BC. (Museum of Fine Arts, Boston. 00.349a)

ARIADNE

CHARACTERS:
Theseus, the son of King Aegeus
Ariadne, the daughter of King Minos
Aegeus, the king of Athens
Minos, the king of Crete
Poseidon
Bacchus
Priest
Seer
Messenger
Water Bearer
Chorus of Maidens
Chorus of Youths
Chorus of Citizens
People

FIRST TABLEAU

THE FOREIGNER

A square in front of the king's palace in Athens. Early dawn. The Messenger is passing by. Near the pond, half reclining, an Old Foreigner. The Water Bearer comes in.

Messenger:
Wake up, he who never slept!
Wake up, he who, like a wandering spirit,
Did not shut his eyes,
Wake up,
The day of mourning is here!

Seven morning stars,
The pride of their forefathers, the joy of their brothers,
Wake up for your journey,
That has no
Return!

Seven valiant lion cubs —
Whose birth and memory will fade —
Together with the maidens,
Wake up. The rope
Is stretched.

Rise, mother's moan,
Over the sea! The earth is awash by the tide.
The ship is prepared.
The law of Athens is —
King Minos!
Wake up, he who is not yet....
(*he passes by*)

Foreigner:

If mortal eyes can from tears
Go blind — there would be no seeing eyes!
What city is it where at night
The babies don't cry — their mothers do?

The old men cry! Something evil has befallen!
The murmur of the sea — like the roar of the lion!
Tell me, water bearer,
Is this city indeed — Athens?

Water Bearer:

None other.

Foreigner:

The smoke of the hearths
Droops. Sacrificial fires should make friends of the heavens!
Maybe you don't worship the gods properly?

Water Bearer:

No, we worship the gods with great zeal.

Day and night, blood and libation
Are poured, generous is the sacrificial incense
In honor of the gray king of the sea,
Poseidon,[1] and of Pallas, the maiden.[2]

Even though they are many, we worship them all!
But tremble, old man, and listen —
For King Aegeus's old fatal sin
A horrible punishment.

Three times eight springs
Ago — to the day — Androgeus, our Cretan
Guest — an archer equal to him
I have never met: from his tongue — thought, birdlike,
Flew, and each thought like an arrow
Hit the target.
His scarlet cloak fluttered.
On his cheeks — youth blooming,
On his lips — wisdom playing.
Brave like a lion, slim like a reed,
Generous as he who with the gods consorts.
Our Cretan guest was always the first
In racing, in wrestling, in throwing the disk,

3

In songs — and in maidens' wistful dreams. . .
— Oh, he would have plucked them by the handful, — had he known! —
But the eternal companion of beauty is
Death — and Androgeus was found
Dead . . . in the splendor of his muscles and charms!
From an arrow shot in his back!
It fell to us to bring to Minos as a gift
His dead young
Son...
          Crete burst out
With war. Awful and many were the sorrows:
Frosts, plagues, droughts, heat
The avenging gods have sent
On our city. The whip of the drought
Burned the harvests, the grasses wither with no juice.
Mothers, weep! The first-born, summon!
The breasts, the grape clusters, the rivers — everything was dried up
In this land —
(pointing to his eyes)
              except for those holes.
The Great Council was called.
To Delphi went the King — to the prophesying stones.
And the answer was clear and stern.
"Androgeus, the joy of the gods,
Is waiting for the sacrifice, not yet sated with blood.
From the white shores of Athens
To the shores of mighty Crete
Let the ship set off. The cargo
Of the ship — is twice seven
Maidens and youths."
                  — The moan of lips
Do you hear? Now to the Cretan shores
For the third time the ship
Is sailing. Once every eight
Springs. That is how Crete
Has punished Athens — for
The very sweetest of all springs. . .
                              The son
Was his father's everything. Day of
Sorrow and ruin! — Aegeus, king of Athens,
Rumor calls a murderer.
Foreigner:
Your king is powerful.
Water Bearer:
                  Sluggish and flabby
Is our king. But sweetness and sorrow — are from above!
Foreigner:
You must atone!

Water Bearer:

                  The third ship!

Foreigner:

    So revolt!

Water Bearer:

            They are coming — do you hear?

    Crying…

Chorus of Maidens:

    O hue of dawn,
    O flower of virginity,
    Hear the groans
    Of seven chosen maidens!

    In anguish and trembling
    Where — miles away —
    Are we sailing?
    Oh, not to the beds of bridegrooms

    Overseas, but to death
    The ship carries us!

Chorus of Youths:

    (*joining in*)
    Seven stars will fade
    Seven roses will wither.

Chorus of Maidens:

    No roses, no lilies, —
    Hades' canopy!
    Seven strings the lyre has —
    And we are seven!

    Blessed are those — whose families grow
    As the lyre plays;
    Seven strings the lyre has —
    And we are seven,

    Sisters in likeness
    Sisters in their spring . . .

Chorus of Youths:

    (*joining in*)
    Seven strings will be broken,
    Seven tears on the oars . . .

Chorus of Maidens:

    O sisters! Confused
    Is the order of the waves.
    Obediently we will step
    On the foaming hill.

    Who is our protector?
    Where is our protector?

We moan in vain,
The end — of our hopes.

Seven maidens, seven gulls
Over the glassy waves...
Chorus of Youths:
(*joining in*)
Seven maidens cast off,
Seven victims sail away.
(*The Chorus of Maidens gives way to the Chorus of Youths.*)
Chorus of Youths:
Tear your solemn garments, tear your hair,
For seven in full bloom...
Set the black sails.
Oarsmen, children of bitterness!

Not towards beautiful maidens, in the kingdom of pleasures,
Not towards monsters, in the kingdom of laurels,
Are seven youths forsaking the shore,
But as a sacrifice for the red Minotaur.

The Minotaur, the fantastic bull,
The accomplice of Minos's revenge,
Our brains and livers he will pierce,
Our chests will he trample with his hooves.

In this way, trampling all the commandments,
Minos takes revenge on us for his son's blood.
Chorus of Maidens:
(*joining in*)
Seven wreaths will fall into dust
Seven tree trunks will bleed to death.
Chorus of Youths:
Oh, if only we could fall under a torrent
Of arrows, so that blood would flow with *laurels*!
We will leave neither offspring, nor deeds,
Nothing, save the plaints of women,

Which only triples the shame:
To fall, without inspiring a single song for the bards!
Chorus of Maidens:
(*joining in*)
Seven warriors lower their shields,
Seven calves offer their necks.
Chorus of Citizens:
Alas, alas!
The young lions will lie on the hot

Gravel — beneath the grass!
The young lions are on the way —
To the slaughterhouse!

Forget, forget,
Mother — those whom you cannot save!
O wind, help
To blow, blow out
The wick

Of futile days . . .
Driving the current astern,
Fiercer, fiercer,
O winds, O winds,
Blow!

What if the noble women
Groan and the wet-nurses weep?
The ship is outfitted.
Athenian law is —
King Minos.

Angrier than an octopus, more evil than a plague…

Foreigner:
Minos? I thought Aegeus was
Your king.

People:
           More trembling than a sacrificial calf — is
Our king.

Foreigner:
           But I thought you stout-hearted,
Not slug-souled!

People:
               Once fallen, stay down.
Why bother?

Foreigner:
           I thought you —
Men!

People:
       We're barely alive, that's what we are. Quit
Preaching. The meat is off the bone.
The price is beyond our strength!

Foreigner:
So are you Minos's herds then,
Not Athenian citizens? Not fathers, you,
But stones? More docile than sheep,
— Moaning, groaning, but where is your sword? —
Awaiting the execution of your hopes?

Beauty dies, yet maturity sleeps?
Shame on you, citizens!

People:

Shame, shame indeed…
To a god — a shrine
To a fish — water
But as for us —
We are beyond shame.

Our lifetime but one hour, our breath but steam . . .

Foreigner:

But you have a king!

People:

Our king is old.

Foreigner:

So what if the king's hair is gray?
He has a son!

People:

One son only
Has our king. Not for us.
Brought up overseas.
Guest in his father's house —
And is he really the king's son?

Hard to tell. There runs a rumor
We heard from the old men and women:
That he is not the king's son,
But an Atlantic guest,
Poseidon's flesh and bone.

But. . . .

Foreigner:

Your story is shady. . .

One of the people:

But why would they care for us,
For such moles of the earth?
And why would we care for them?
For gods, for kings
And for their sons?...

They fan the flame
But our kin go to death!

People:

Alas, alas!
The young lions will lie on the far
Cliff — beneath the grass.
The young lions are sailing. . .

Foreigner:

> Enough!
>
> With the turn of the rudder
> The bet can be settled. With the call of bonfires
> Summon the king!
> Let the lot be cast.
>
> Let the sail of the fatal ship
> Trouble the king's heart, too!
> He is not childless — lead out
> Your son! He is a youth — not an infant!
>
> The son is twice responsible
> For his father's ashes and royal crimson.
> Let him stand along with your son,
> Meeker than a white ram.
>
> As the king stands as father to many,
> It is not right that he guards one only.
> Like the waves beneath the oars,
> So is the grass underneath an indifferent sickle.
>
> In the time of harvest and war
> All are equal. In blood and in bread —
> All are Aegeus's sons!
>
> Everything else the lot decides.
>
> King! — Come, sing along!
> King! — Come, roll out your voices!
> King! — Three commandments
> You must honor.
>
> You have no kin,
> You have no strangers,
> Forgetful King!
> And here is the third verse
>
> Of this commandment . . .
> — King! — Shake
> The walls! Come on, fight!
> I am the god! Why am I waiting?!
>
> Where they delay
> The commandments —
> The gods interfere
> In the game.

People

> To the king! To the king!
> Into the palace!

Foreigner:

> > Come on, push, all together!

People:

> Father! Father
> Aegeus! Give us Theseus!
> The arrow is shot!
> Suffer like we suffer!
> (*Aegeus appears*)

Aegeus:

> Greetings to you,
> Athenian citizens.
>
> What brings you to my house
> At the hour of morning darkness?

People:

> We could not wait,
> King! The sea is uneasy!
> The wave is rising!
> The tide of blood erupted and ebbed.

Aegeus:

> What generosity are you
> Expecting here?

People:

> > We are here for your
> Son! If *you* are
> Silent — the stones came alive!
> We, too, are fathers!
> — And first-borns have we as well
> In our houses! Over the edge
> Is this sorrow! Or else — in ruins
> Your palace! Give us
> Theseus for the lottery like everyone else!
> (*shouting*)
> Theseus! If he is indeed the
> King's son, he won't cower!
> Give us Theseus, Athens's
> Hope!

Aegeus:

> > So listen:
> I agree!
> (*to someone in the palace*)
> > > Prepare the ship
> With the black sail!
> I am giving you
> Theseus,
> The pillar of my old age…

People:
Bring him out!

Words are simply futile!
Let the lot decide
On this very square!
We ask for Theseus!

Aegeus:
In front of my eyes

Let the shrine of my soul
Come out at once —
My last hope
I surrender to you,
Athens!

People:
Long live the

King! Glory to the king!
Indeed you are our king!

Aegeus:

If the lot, which is blind,
Falls on my only offspring,
You won't be left hingeless,
O golden gates of Athens.

Fear neither plagues, nor evils, —
Not in vain does the king get along with his people!
The fifty sons of Pallas
Will inherit my throne.

Pallas, my terrible brother.
Do not fear the crack in the throne!
Instead of one true-blooded king
Fifty are promised you,
Mighty, tall…

People:
But the brothers will start

Fighting! We will see neither the crumbs nor the crust
From the pie!

Aegeus:
Fifty pillars for the

Kingdom!

People:
Or maybe fifty kites? [3]

Aegeus:

So take my son over the sea:
My son: my life and my eyes!
You won't be left without a king!
Take Theseus overseas,

To the Minotaur.

People
>   The king is ready.
> But will we be safer?
> All in all fifty fathers!
> All in all fifty kings!
>
> Brother against brother: strike and burn!
> The blizzard that blindly rolls!
> Brother against brother: whip and sword!
> We all are but their stepsons!
>
> And as stepfathers they will plunder
> The kingdom! — The most horrible of all servitudes!
> The itch of fifty sores!
> The roar of fifty quarrels!
>
> We are promised a dragon
> With fifty heads!
> Faster, faster across the waves,
> We do not need Theseus!

Aegeus:
> My word has been spoken. A mooring-rope
> Is the king's oath — alone!

People:
> It's the foreigner's fault!

Aegeus:
> The king's oath — is given.
>
> The rope does not follow
> The whims of a flighty sail.

People:
> It's the foreigner's fault!
> You — fooled us, you — stirred us up,
>
> You urged us on! Bind
> The evil seer! We are all faithful
> To Aegeus! Stay back,
> Guest from Hades' realm.
>
> You fell on our heads like
> Thunder! It is our turn now!
> How can the hands work apart from the mind,
> And a people apart from its king?
>
> — Citizens! Am I right?
> — Into custody! — Onto the block!
> — Pluck his sting out!
> — Burn him alive!

— Crush him!
— In chains down to his heels!
(Theseus appears)

Theseus:

Keep your hands off!
A foreigner is sacred!

Citizens, in this kingdom
Guests and old men
Are revered.
I do not recognize

In this uneven fight —
My glorious homeland!

Insulting a guest?

People:

Lies are in him, and evil.

Theseus:

Whoever he is, or is not —
He is an old man and a guest.

On an old man — you take revenge?

People:

Poison's in him, and harm.

Theseus:

Twice sacred:
Stranger and old man.

People:

Against our foundations
He went and is exposed!

Theseus:

Respect the stranger,
That is your law!

People:

A knife is prepared
Against your life!

Theseus:

Respect the gray hair —
Here is Theseus for you!

An old man — into custody?
A guest — to the authorities?

Aegeus:

But against you yourself,
My son, has he rebelled!

Theseus:

I know. I have no fear
Of being immortal.

> To Minos as a sacrifice
> I surrender myself!

> In the ship at once
> I sail with you — without a lottery.

Aegeus:
> My son!

Theseus:
> I await
> The king's blessing.

Aegeus:
> I am old.

Theseus:
> But I am
> Passionate — and in the ranks
> Of Athenian citizens —
> Am first. — Let us sail!

Aegeus:
> I am weak.

Theseus:
> But your son has enough
> Strength for two.

People:
> Glory to Theseus!
> The new Heracles! [4]

Aegeus:
> My son! The wolves
> In the hills are kinder!
> Yield to me!

Theseus:
> I can't yield.
> For the brave — are the wreaths! [5]

Aegeus:
> Into custody the stubborn one.

Theseus:
> To your oars, oarsmen!

> Sail,
> To the sea!

People:
> O joy!

Aegeus:
> O sorrow!

Theseus:
> Be smooth, sea's abyss!

People:
> Glory to the king's son!

Aegeus:
> Then choke

On your father's blood.
You, your father's murderer!

Foreigner:

(*stepping up*)
Halt
The words in your throat,
And the anger on your lips.
The young one is relentless.
The youth is right.
(*To Theseus*)
My son! We still
Need passions!
You are a chosen son
Of Poseidon.

In any dream and in any guise
Far and near,
Thrice call —
Thrice will I respond.

The gray in my hair is the foam,
The angry waves.
Thrice ask of me —
Thrice I will fulfill.

Fall on my chest,
My son, confirmed in his glory.
(*hugs him*)
Waves, billow! Winds, blow!

People:

(*prostrating themselves*)
Lord Poseidon!

SECOND TABLEAU

THESEUS AT MINOS'S PALACE

The throne room of Minos on Crete. Ariadne, alone, playing with a ball.

Ariadne:

Higher, higher! Piercing the roof —
To the Olympians, into the modeled blue of heaven!
My ball of thread, golden and smooth.
The gift of the most beautiful of goddesses!

It has great hidden powers,
The thread is steady and shiny.

The mistress Aphrodite
Giving it to me uttered:

"The man to whom you hand this —
Along with your fate, along with your will —
He amid all fetters will remain free,
He amid all intrigues will remain innocent.

All thresholds for him are open roads!
Even in his passions he will remain clearsighted."
But with the sacred ball meanwhile
Ariadne still plays.

"Hide away the golden
Gift of the bride! . . "
From mortal earth fly
Higher, higher, my magic ball!

"Do not give it to anyone until the time comes,
Many are dear, only one is dearest!"
So she taught, bending
Over her favorite maiden.

"Do not hand it to anyone if you don't yearn
To please him until his hair turns gray,
For every woman on this earth
There is only one among the chosen.

Hide away the golden
Gift of the bride! . . "
Fly far up away from the mortal soil,
My magic ball.

Aphrodite from my earliest years
Caressed me: like a mother
Her child. "Your chosen man
Will not fail to be mine as well.

Only in his loyalty he must be tested,
In his loyalty he must be great —
I will shower him with every favor
All his roads — all on time!

So that he can fly like an earthly god,
Laurel and joy on his young forehead..."
But alas, this golden glossy
Ball — as always, to my palm

Returns. My bridal gift
Always — from my intended. I want to cry!
Come, my ball, fly higher, higher
Away from this earth!

But here is the clank of bronze!
But here is the crimson of armor!
But here is the burning of bloody torches!
Now my play is at an end.
Greetings to you, my king and father!

Minos:

(*surrounded by his torchbearers*)
What have you been doing
In this bare throne room, daughter?

Ariadne:

I was playing.

Minos:

Games are but ghosts, joy is but sound.
With what were you playing?

Ariadne:

By beating my quick hands
I was testing the swift ball.

Minos:

In the place of my putrid sorrow?
On the day most grievous, most evil?

Ariadne:

But maidens know nothing of past days!

Minos:

The whole land is trembling and crying!

Ariadne:

I was tossing my bouncy ball,
That it might bring me some joy!
Maidens do not know drawn-out tears!

If you cry forever — the tears will be all drained!
How long can a seed stay in its pod?
A sigh over a future bridegroom is sweeter
Than a sigh over a dead brother!

Minos:

There is no heart in your breast!

Ariadne:

I never knew
Sorrow.

Minos:

On the eve of my downfall!
Now is the eve of his death!

Ariadne:

But your first-born, my king, *was* young,

I *now* am. And already I have three
Times eight springs, father!

Minos:

Age stands still.
He was given to me only once.

Ariadne:

But maidens do not have old wounds!
Only new ones! Say that I am like green grass —
How long is its life?
It is already tomorrow — and without tomorrow
A maiden is like today without
Yesterday. Short is the day of our beauty!

Minos:

He was only once given to me, but taken every hour since,
Taken every evening, every night.

Ariadne:

But if a son-in-law comes to replace the son
Perhaps, the grove's manly treetop will grow again?

Minos:

How can a son-in-law replace a son?

Ariadne:

Well, yet I remain,
The solace of your old age.

Minos:

A daughter is no son.
A daughter, — alas! — a fine substitute! —
For a son! A stronghold — for foam
Exchanging? In this sea of tears
A girl is foam, a son is a rock.

Do not complain to a man undone.

Ariadne:

A son is a rock, but a daughter is created to be
Joy, a butterfly in your dwelling.

Minos:

The sacrificial ship is slow to arrive!
I will assess a triple tribute from them!
For a moment of delay
— This anger turns me into a butcher —
Groves of brave youths and canopies of maidens!

Triple profit for the Minotaur.

Messenger:

King, the long-awaited ship is here.
Some youth is at my heels,
With a masterful temper.

18

Theseus:

> (*entering*)
>
>   The guest enters of his own accord
>
> — If awaited.
> (*to Minos*)
> Hello, priest
> thrice-cursed!
> I am no bard:
> I will be brief.
> So double your wits.
> I am the leader of the boat of the condemned.
> I am the eighth. Nothing more.
> — Not by lot, but by free will
> Am I here to lay myself down, an evening sacrifice
> For Athens.
>   — Take my sword!
> (*gives Minos his sword*)
> It is plenty wet
> With evil blood.
> I am no bridegroom:
> I will be urgent.
>
> From Aegeus's evil arrow
> Fell your first-born. — Eagles
> Fall so! — For Androgeus, fallen in groans,
> Here is Theseus — in ransom!
>
> For Aegeus's horrible sin
> The son will answer — one for all.

Minos:

> Son?!

Theseus:

>   Kill me,
> Let the sword
> Gleam crimson.

Minos:

> (*stepping forward*)
>   Theseus?
> Son of Aegeus?
> (*their glances duel*)
> ...Yet of all the people I know
> Only *you* would have looked back at me!
> (*with renewed rage*)
> Son of the murderer!?
> (*to the guards*)
> Take this swindler away from me!

Theseus:

> King, I haven't finished my tale yet!
> When you see the crimson of my blood,

19

King, remove the fatal ransom
From the sinful city. . .

Minos:

(*to the guards*)
Take away this madman!

Theseus:

I am not mad, come to your senses,
You! I am flinging my life to you
As a generous gift. Isn't that enough?

My blood, which eternity would never have dried up! [6]
The glory of a future Heracles!
Hecatombs that the world
Has not yet seen! Myriads of deeds
Undone and undoable.
Ask the gods in high heaven,
The gods in the depths of the oceans
Ask.
     Waterfalls of odes,
King, as into an abyss,
I am throwing!
For the worst thing that I am losing
This day — is not the air, not the sense in my fingers,
But the echo of song in the chests of bards!

King, I will go down unknown. For
Is it a really a skill — nailing Procrustes[7] to his bed of death?
I have tried the young swing of my fist
On vagabonds and boars,
But I have never slaughtered
A single Chimaera…
          But trust me,
King: a singular man, not just anyone,
Tomorrow will be led
To slaughter. It will be the one, the only one.
Blood equal to Androgeus's will flow.

Minos:

          What likeness!
Did Hades[8] call up a ghost?
Thus in the muted ashes
Of the hearth — an unmeltable diamond:
Honor.
     Theseus with Androgeus, — you are right!
These *mountains* are equal in the scales.
About the youths and maidens
Do not fret. On the blue seaway
To them I will entrust the urn
With your famous ashes — and the news,
That here on Crete — we, too, have hearts.

We will not repay with a treacherous arrow
Our guest. It would be more just as a son-in-law
To receive you into my house. Here, take her!
To give you my throne! To fill to the brim
The wedding goblets,
To call you my everything!

Theseus:

                         King, come to your senses!

Minos:

I would find once more sleep and conscience…

Theseus:

But between you and me — the blood
Of Androgeus!

Minos:

(*confused*)

               Blood, where is it?...

Theseus:

We are citadels
Of two warring shores!

Minos:

                    Sleep I would find, and laughter…
But *their* will must be fulfilled!

Theseus:

King, do not delay the hour of
Doom!

Minos:

          He will be but cattle for slaughter! A pile of flesh!
A mess of twitches and shudders!
And not at some point sometime, somewhere, but here,
Tomorrow, even . . .

Theseus:

          Do not be crushed! I have no regrets.

Minos:

But now there is still time. . . still. . .
— That look that broke me like a stick! —
But now, now, you are still my
Guest!
         My source of fresh water in the desert!
A ghost! My first-born! The trace of a signet ring
On wax (which I thought was marble!)
Of my old heart.

Theseus:

King, do not delay the fatal hour!

Minos:

Daughter, give our guest
A golden goblet. Fill it to the brim,
For it is full of tears.
               — Drink and sleep.

(The same hall. Night. Theseus alone).

Theseus:

> The winged stroke of my heart,
> The fraught groan of the wave,
> Midnight and blood in my ears —
> Everything chases my sleep away.
>
> The drawn-out call of the night guard,
> The empty refrain of the sea-foam
> Upon far-away islands full of prey —
> Everything inflames my anger.
>
> Wrath on you, O strength,
> That gave this oath:
> To lie down like a ram to slaughter.
> Like a slavewoman tossing my sword into the night.
>
> Wrath on you, O hand!
> (Easier it is to separate
> Boar's tusks — than these fingers!) that gave as
> Tribute my honor.
>
> Wrath on you, O luxury
> Of my sinews! Having been
> Close to the gods, with no sword now,
> I am but a reed in a swamp! Not a man.
>
> Wrath on you, O voice,
> Of tree, of grass, of brook:
> "That man who saved Athens,
> Without drawing his sword!"
>
> I will close my eyes in lamenting,
> Vanquished without a fight!
> There *is* no name for this anger
> Other than: shame.
>
> I will go down lamenting to Hades'
> Underground shrine of glory,
> There *is* no name for this deed
> Other than: disgrace.
> *(enter Ariadne)*

Ariadne:

> My speech will be brief:
> I have brought you a thread and a sword.
>
> So that the hospitality of the Cretan maiden
> May live through the centuries.

With this sword you will strike the bull,
With this thread — you will get out of the labyrinth.

That's all, now sleep.
                              Go back to your homeland
Safe and sound!

Theseus:
A goddess you seem to me,
But I can't accept your gifts.

Ariadne:
Guest, come to your senses!

Theseus:
                              I swore an oath
To appear unarmed, my face uncovered.

Ariadne:
Your sword, with which Procrustes was killed!

Theseus:
Between sword and my hand — the oath
Of my lips. The raising of my right hand!
There is honor between hand and hilt —
Honor, the most pitiless of ropes.
I am captive to my own given oath.

Ariadne:
Obedience does not suit you!

Theseus:
I do not prostrate myself vanquished,
I surrender to Minos by my own free will!

Ariadne:
Remember *your own* father,
He is old and old age is unstable!
Who will cherish his last days
If not his first-born son?

Theseus:
                              There is a power
More pitiless than a father's honor.

May destiny be fulfilled.

Ariadne:
By Androgeus's features
Mesmerized, my father will forgive!

Theseus:
Honor — the most pitiless of plaintiffs.

Ariadne:
There is no evil force in the universe
Equal to the Minotaur's.

Theseus:
                              Wounded
Honor is a hundred times more monstrous
Than the Minotaur.

Ariadne:

                    Neither right, nor holy
Is this deed! You are already great!
For the sake of this my trembling
Smile — renounce! Slay!
For the sake of this my gushing
Tear! If the scales are flawed
Does a man's oath have weight?

Theseus:

There is in this life a power
More pitiless than beauty: honor.

In vain do you struggle and in vain do you try.

Ariadne:

Enlighten the blasphemer,[9]
Gods! Fall, proud one, from your mountain!
These are Aphrodite's gifts.

The mirror of her highest will,
I am here only as her messenger,
Only to utter her will
Have I brought you thread and sword.

But I know in advance the answer
Of your lips inflamed with delirium:
"The most pitiless power is that of
Divinity over man."

Theseus:

(*bowing to her*)

                Nay.[10]

THIRD TABLEAU

LABYRINTH

The entrance to the Labyrinth. Enter Ariadne.

Ariadne:

In vain above this solidity
Do both ear and groan struggle.
Louder does sand in an hourglass
Flow, more noisily does Charon

Strike the Stygian water with his oar.
My brother, whose days are over,
Louder over your onyx urn
Does the laurel spread its shadow.

ARIADNE

He vanished, and vanished completely!
Yield, my straining hearing!
Louder does a shadow raise
Its finger on a sundial.

Will I again see him
Who is like a god to me?
The offspring of Daedalus[11] will not respond;
It gives no secrets to the day.

Oh, the bitterness of weakness!
My God — who did not know you!
Daedalus, who set the stones so closely,
Be accursed!

Vault which heeds nobody!
Dead is he who wanders within you!
An accumulation of weaknesses —
Be accursed, my sex!

Deep is the river
Of maidenly intuitions.
Do not let go of the thread,
Do not let fall the spool!

I strain to hear — but like the inside of an urn
All is muffled, like in widows' wombs.
I strain to hear — as into an urn,
I strain to see — as into a ditch…

Louder does a tree seep its resin,
Louder is the dew on bushes . . .
I strain to see — as into the maw
Of a lion's dark yawn.

What is there, around the corner?
Better not to see, not to hear!
Is the whole spool unwound?
The silence of the stone blocks is treacherous.

Was the bull covered with blood, with foam
When he fell? Or was he[12] stricken in his forehead by a horn?
The scream of my feelings
Is as unreliable as the muteness of these stone blocks.

Praise to Aphrodite,
Amid thunders and in silence!
Do not let go of the thread!
Do not let fall the soul!

Aphrodite!
Myrtle and honey!
The entire defense,
The whole entire bulwark

For the most zealous of Cretan women,
In this darkest of traps,
Aphrodite, be a ray of light,
To the man of the bright face!

Aphrodite!
Journey and goal!
Flax through flagstones,
Light through a crack,

Joining the lions with a flaxen thread,
Let him enter and let him exit,
For the guileless soul,
Aphrodite, be a path!

Aphrodite!
Salt! wave!
If a ransom
Is needed — here!

Spare his life for great deeds,
Take mine as ransom instead!
He appeared as a lion, as a sun!
Aphrodite! Maiden!...

He has fallen! Sound like a hammer,
A hammer's noise and thud!
A mighty one has fallen! But who?
The warrior or the bull?

This is not a block tumbling,
Not the river down from a cliff headlong!
Thusly only the body
Of warrior or bull!

Thusly — kingdoms crash down!
Into the dust — beam upon beam!
The heavenly vault is shaken,
Rivers leap out of their beds!

On his stern-browed forehead
Is that blood or a halo?
The labyrinth has spoken
Its words into eternity.

My heart, be manly,
Manly and hopeful!
The heavenly vault is broken!
In the trembling of birds' flocks,

In the rumbling retinue of wings,
Roses in her wake . . .
Aphrodite is coming
The heavenly…

Theseus:
> (*on the threshold of the labyrinth*)
> — Light!

Ariadne:
> Alive?

Theseus:
> Let us go,
> Maiden!

Ariadne:
> Dream!
> Alive?

Theseus:
> Victorious!

Ariadne:
> Bull?

Theseus:
> Slaughtered!

Ariadne:
> Whole?

Theseus:
> Whole-heartedly
> Received death.

Ariadne:
> Whole?

Theseus:
> Immortal.

Ariadne:
> Sword?

Theseus:
> Bloody.
> Maiden, let us go!

Ariadne:
> Guest, have a drink!
> Whole, but pale…

Theseus:

    No more chains!

    My city is free!

    Winds, blow

    For my way homeward!

Ariadne:

    Guest, please stay!

Theseus:

    The sword is crimson!

    The sail is full!

Ariadne:

    Guest, a goblet!

Theseus:

    Maiden, to the ship!

Ariadne:

    Guest, please wait!

    The widow's bread is

    Cruel.

Theseus:

        So let's go,

    My life!

Ariadne:

        Alas!

    (*begins singing*)

    My guest — you sail far!

    In fable and in song — you will have fame.

    The maiden — will be forgotten.

    The guest — will forget.

Theseus:

    Your words are dark

    Explain

    Their meaning.

Ariadne:

        Far

    Is your sailing! Through dreams

    Of days, alongside the foam under your keel

    You will drag with you

    My face and my trace.

    But the whole world

    Is too little for you!

Theseus:

        So let's go,

    Maiden!

Ariadne:

        No.

Theseus:

    The spirit is forged

    In sorrows and storms.

    I am ignorant of maidens,

To their babblings I am deaf.

Go right or go left,
Go uphill or down!

Ariadne:
Ah, a maiden — is a cryptic text:
You need the key.

Theseus:
I grew up and became strong
As red granite.
I am no dream interpreter,
I am blind to foresights.

I am hardened as old coal,
I am a man, not fluff!

Ariadne:
A maiden is an intention:
You need to hear.

Theseus:
I heard, but I don't understand.
Quit singing a nightingale's song!
I have no use for fables,
Nor am I strong in flattery.

If you love — then follow
Into light and into darkness!

Ariadne:
A maiden is a curtain:
A signal is needed.

Theseus:
Virginity's timidity?
Nature's
Cry? Answer me,
My life! Is it pity
For your father? I respect your sadness, —
But your father cannot lose his life twice!
With his son, all the iron left his veins.
He is dead — once and for all.

Would your brother
Appear everywhere to you?
Yes, I am begotten
By a murderer!
But we will stop the ghosts
Creeping to our bed!
Between *that* and our passion
Is a sword. Rising from our
Passionate bonds — I will
Slaughter that ghost!

There is nothing in my heart —
Except for
Kind thoughts. Are you shy?
Or is it your family's honor?
But I swear to you twice over
Not as a mere delight but as a wife,
The mother of my future offspring,
You will enter my house, sacred from now on.

Maiden! Do you hear, the wave
Rages against the rigging!
Maiden! My passion
Groans as a lioness!
Punish for my audacious guess:
But is the trembling of this bosom
For someone else?
Is the hem of your garment
For someone else's daring hands?

Ariadne:
                                        Don't torture me!
Guest, your sailing is far!
A handful from Lethe you'll drink,
Guest! Covered in ashes —
The maiden will be forgotten.

Guest, let's finish
The bitter talk.
The wave is your helmsman!

Theseus:
The deep — our chorus!

Ariadne:
Take away my bliss —
Young man!
                    It is not the shameful quarrel
Of woman's passion with her reason, no.
Nor is it a gray-haired father's
Dark grief, nor the now faded
Stains of fraternal blood, —
Yet still crimson! —
Nor yet the cloying blend
Of timidity and faintheartedness
Called firmness,
Called maiden's honor.

Theseus:
                                        Enough
Arguing, then!

Ariadne:
(*raising her hand*)
                        Sword of retribution!

30

Great futility of prayers!
I was chosen by Aphrodite
As her favorite, by the sweetest
Of mistresses! After prey —
The most zealous! In love —
The most furious!
                    Sail,
Guest! While you are only a brother to me —
Go! While your path —
Mirror of mirrors! — is unbounded,
Go! While you do not know
My lips...
                For like a stone
Is my passion! For my passion
Is your ruin! For
What was promised to me
Will be exacted from you
Not by a mortal daughter, but by that one
Who makes flax out of the wild beasts.[13]

Guest, far is your sailing!
You have to weave some new nets,
Guest! Love others,
Forget this one.

Since you have not yet seen the whole world,
My brother, come to your senses!
There are so many sweet maidens!
But roses wither —
All of them.

Theseus:
                Deluded one!

Ariadne:
                        The deluded one is —
You. The gods watch over all oaths
For a single glance aside — O child of the children
of Aphrodite! — You will pay
With everything.

Theseus:
                Sooner into the sea
Will the headlands move!

Ariadne:
                        Oh, do not give oaths,
Guest! Are the threads of your fate
Known to you? The shore is dangerous not only
Because of maidens —
There are jungles, and caves of delights,

The midnight grottos of *those* pleasures.
Can you know what awaits you
Around the corner? The bosoms of
Nymphs and goddesses —
Are they not also a labyrinth?

In the most hidden of temples,
Guest, you will seize immortality with
Your sinews. Invincible is
The ardor of the gods
For mortals. Do not measure yourself against the immortals,
Young man! The most terrible punishment —
Is the passion of immortality for death!
Who can dare to reject the gift of a goddess —
Her lips, her loveliness?

Theseus:
                                        I can dare!
Sooner will the headland
Budge from its place!

Ariadne:
                                Oh, don't give oaths,
Young man!

Theseus:
                        Let the light of my eyes
Darken!

Ariadne:
                        Do you know that
Gods have loved mortal maidens
Before?
(*touching the laurel tree*)
                        These leaves
Still tremble with Daphne's
Quivering …
                                If you become my husband,
If you give a vow to me — even in your dreams,
How can you, mere ashes,
Measure up to a god?
Can you venture to lift
The burden of an outcast or a sacrilege?
Will you enter hand against hilt
Into a fight with a dweller of Mount Parnassus?[14]
Will you venture to be renowned,
Mortal man, as an outcast and as a god-fighter?

Guest, your sailing is far!
To respect inhuman
Will — is to serve the gods.
You must forget the maiden.

You can't buy pleasure
With the price of Tartarus.
You will back off! You will yield to
One above!

Theseus:
                I have only one power over me —
My passion!

Ariadne:
                You will trample your passion.
I am afraid to be your
Darling. It is more obvious
Than a snake's bite: I will be tossed aside
By this man! Smoke —
Is your passion. Fire from wood shavings
Is your passion! You can't serve two masters,
Mortal man! There is no fate and no kin to a man
Except the immortal gods!

Away, passion is not a pasture but a wasteland!
You will give way! You will give up!
You will give out! Like a flower
You will let me fall!

Theseus:
                What illness
Is burning you?

Ariadne:
                But the Foam-born[15]
Has bones that remember. You will be
Indentured to her, if you touch my lips.
Do you know that her eyes are empty,
And without slack is
Her chain!

Theseus:
                I will snatch you away from Zeus
Himself! From right before his eyes
I will snatch you away!

Ariadne:
                Do not give oaths,
Guest! You are only a reed
Swayed by the wind. The cluster of my coveted
Vine. The nail of all my live
Veins. The bridegroom of my soul. . .

Stop! As you broke faith with Minos —
For more weighty than all Minos's cordialities —
Is the sign of their eyes…oh! So will you dissolve marriage
To his sweet daughter. Guest of wide lands,

It is not for you to lie with me
In the thickets…

Theseus:
Then — on my sword!
(*His gesture is interrupted by the youths and maidens*)
Chorus of Youths and Maidens:
Brother will I see!
Mother will I see!
Harvest will I see!
Glory to Theseus!

Sword at rest!
Groan ripped out!
Seven-seas wind,
Glory to the bull-fighter!

Swift oars, steep rigging,
Glory to the homeland's liberator!
Glorify, O fleeing stern,
The man who did not submit to the yoke!

Set the sails,
Helmsman! Southward!
The sin is atoned!
The stone is lifted!
I will be a sweetheart
And a wife,
And I will rock my children to sleep!

Set a straighter course,
Helmsman! With the splash
Of the oars, from the waves to high heaven:
Honor to Theseus,
Who has returned us — to our brides,
And our brides — to us!

Hail to you, brave man!
You lifted off a mountain!
Hail to you, kind man!
Olympus still lives!
Minos is overthrown
With the Minotaur!
The labyrinth's spell is broken!

Steer more bravely,
Helmsman! Crete
Is broken! We will fall asleep free!

Honor to Theseus,
Who returned to us — the law,
And the law — to us!

Hail!

Theseus:
> Onward!

Ariadne:
> Don't leave me!

Theseus:
> Winds, blow!

Ariadne:
> Be faithful.

Theseus:
> Maiden goddesslike
> In your beauty, what is your name?

Ariadne:
> Ariadne.

FOURTH TABLEAU

NAXOS

Ariadne is sleeping on a cliff.

Theseus:
> (*over the sleeping Ariadne*)
> She sleeps, having learned
> The hidden truth of souls.
> She sleeps, with pleasure sated,
> Sleep! — Your husband keeps watch.
>
> Branch, carried by a current!
> Passion — respect her, she sleeps!
> I am sleepless only because
> I am not sated with pleasure.
>
> Does not the nightingale keep watch,
> Gripped by the same bitterness?
> As if I am drinking up the sea,
> With each hour — ever saltier!
>
> She sleeps, crumbling as a rose,
> In the surge of fierce caresses,
> How soon was she sated
> With my hunger!

Even if like a pearl into the deep
She vanishes, — I will catch her in my palm!
Sleep, young woman!
The blood remembers.

Ariadne:

(*in her sleep*)

I love!

Theseus:

Through the clinging honeysuckle
Of dreams — hear the verdict:
The earthly is slaked in us,
The immortal — is not.

Bottomless is our vat of aspirations,
Our thoughts higher than our forehead!
Bodies can be sated,
Our yearning is deathless!

Like a lifeless warrior, —
No sigh in her breast, —
She sleeps. But know, that anew
The strife will blaze up…

Ariadne:

(*in her sleep*)

Love!

Theseus:

Through the damasked curtain
Of sleep — with my heart I will get through.
The soul in us is tireless,
And lips are not enough for her,[16]

And not enough for her the mirror
Of *those* games and pleasures.
Sleep, young mortal woman.
Death will pass by.

Ariadne:

(*in her sleep*)

Forever.

Theseus:

Her bloom will fade, her figure
Will hunch, her roses — will be gone, breeze-borne!
Against death and destiny
Even Zeus — is no stronghold.

And — a bed, harder than this rocky
Couch — is prepared for us.
But — in reality and in truth —
Know: our passion will stand strong.

(*raising his right hand*)
Maiden of low places and recesses,
In caves and in thickets
Reigning, — hear my
Oath over this sleeping woman.

In the holiness of marriage ties
With my dear honeysuckle
Will I twine myself — I swear it
By the waters of the Styx.

I swear by the cloudy
Brows of Olympus
To shun the dewy lips
Of maid and nymph.

Fates and mouths having twinned,
Right up to death's
Bite...
      — By the wrath
Of your loins, I swear:

Even *you* are not more eternal
Than my passion!
And if ever in the darkness of
Feeling, mind, vitals,

I break this wondrous union, —
Let your wrath be surety! —
Let me then forget the taste
Of milk and of oil!

Oh, let treacherous sleep
Flee my eyes!
Let baldness instead of laurel
Mark my brow!

Let my bronze helmet fall into the dust!
Let me fall like a coward!
Let my forehead never touch
My father's threshold!

Let me never touch the gray hair
Of my father! Let me never see her
Heavy with offspring! Nor
See my children!

Oh, let me then learn
The price of trampled oaths!

Let me then learn the coldness of women,
The betrayal of a friend!

Let women's intrigues
Compel me to spin flax![17]
Let passion mock
My late old age!

Let then my father-in-law
Mock his former son-in-law!
Let me know the flattery of servants,
The division of the kingdom!

Let the water never run
Into the vessels of water bearers!
Let the fertile fields
Never bear fruit!
(*Leaning over the sleeping Ariadne*)
Be it Zeus himself
Together with the Fates —
I will never take off these irons!
(*Light. From the light — a Voice*)

Voice:
To Bacchus — you will yield.

Theseus:
The sound charming my heart —
Echoes like a cithara in my ears.[18]
Who are you?

Voice:
I am the son of a maiden and the Almighty,
The predestined bridegroom
Of your bride. Sweeter than drinking
Milk on the sweetest of beds —
Is the woman resting here,
Intended for me from forever.

Theseus:
You lie!
This sword is still wet with the
Minotaur's blood.
You will come to know how heavy is
Theseus's hand.

Voice:
Hush ... Sleep
Is not deep in the presence of divinity.

Theseus:
If you are not a phantom, not carved in stone,
Come out, — let us know each other, idle talker!

Voice:
I beseech you again —
The trembling cover of her sleep is fragile!

38

Have mercy, neither father nor house
Has she.

Theseus:

        Let's fight then,
Insolent one!

Voice:

        Be silent! Respect the slumber
Of the maiden dreaming about you.

They love — think you? No, they hack
Thus! No, — they destroy! No, — they tear veins!
Oh, how little, how badly they love!
They love, they hack — a single deadly

Sound! Do you call this
Love? Play of the sinews —
Nothing more! More wooden than a log
And more clumsy than an ax.

Oh, how dull and awkward:
Bed — bonds — spurious heat of blood…
The maiden, who learned what a husband is,
Sleeps, sleeps through

The braziers of your intoxication. From such disgraces
Valleys are turned upside down and rivers flow back!
Like eating sweet fruit to remove bitterness,
The maiden droops — to smother in sleep

Your caresses. Meeker than a fallen nag!
Fallen like one dead! A spasm across her mouth —
Of your marriage and nuptials
This is the most revolting vanity.

Oh, how little and how unskillfully
You caress!

Theseus:

        Unveiler of brows,
Who are you?

Voice:

        I am the fiery son of Semele —
The terrifying god of inspiration.

Theseus:

Bacchus!

Voice:

        The double-hearted and the double-depthed.

Theseus:

Bacchus!

Voice:

        Kept warm in the male womb.[19]

Theseus:

    Bacchus!

Voice:

        Born not of a woman.

Theseus:

    Bacchus!

Voice:

        But twice having seen the light.

    The one whose doubleness doubles
    The glance of everyone who has seen clearly.

Theseus:

    Bacchus!

Voice:

        The enlarged frontier.

Theseus:

    Bacchus!

Voice:

        Limit of your limits.

    The one whose spirit you drink
    In round-dances and on hill-tops.
    That god who in battle fraternizes
    With the evil convicts of the flesh.

    The leader of the thunderous chorus,
    — All who thirst, come hither! —
    I am the god who bestows gifts indiscriminately,
    And who erases without a trace.

    I am the scourge of hypocrites,
    Who stand aloof! I am the grumble in your ears, the roar which
    To those below — is fright and stupor,
    To those above — is the tongue of command!

    Oh, there is no *up to* me, no beyond me!
    I have no nets and no bonds!
    I am insatiable, I hunger for famine:
    Only thirst slakes me.

    I am the double-depthed, the twice-born,
    The double-faithed, — both leader and guard…
    And there will indeed be a pitcher for the thirst
    Of this maiden, dying of thirst amid

    Goblets…

           With a winged flutter of the eyelids
These roses will become ashes.
Smoothed out now as if by a chisel,
These eyebrows will become moss.

The trustful meekness of this forehead
Experience will plow
With evil furrows. The satin of the cheeks
Will be all furrowed with veins, as if

With a pitchfork! Having birthed a smile —
Weep! No — prolong it: for the same worm
Gnaws away at any fruit:
Sorrow dries you up, pleasure burns,

Everything is shortweighted! Think you that this is —
A miracle? All that is, is maggot-eaten,
Man!

Theseus:
                 I break with the obvious!

Bacchus:
        (*who till the end remains only a voice*)
Death — is the maggot's name.

The sapling never blossoms twice!
Youth cannot slow
The sprightly buskin.[20] You think
You are protecting the maiden? Rather, an urn

Of ashes! You set yourself to fight a god, —
Drawn by a ghost! A shadow!
A tiny handful of dust
That was once a flower!

Tell me, has anything sweeter
Bloomed, on the heights of the mountains,
On azure riversides? It is up to you
To cut short or to make immortal

This blossom. Greedier than the Minotaur,
Angrier than Zeus's thunder
Is the fire of creaturely fury
Called passion. Conquer it!

Yield, although deeply in love,
The maiden to the god

Of the hops-curly head!

Theseus:

> The maiden won by me!
> By sword and by devotion. . .

Bacchus:

> The maiden destined for me!
>
> For centuries foreseen!
> Mine, without sharing!
> As the vine to the vine-dresser,
> So is this maiden to me!
>
> Does divinity with nothingness
> Argue? Meager-hearted man,
> What can you offer her as a wedding gift?
> Old age and death?
>
> Beauty and deathlessness —
> There in the double-depthed basin
> Of the bridegroom-cupbearer
> The gift for the bride: for her soul.
>
> Theseus's gift and Bacchus's
> Tribute — I put on the scales.
> Weigh them. Are they really of equal
> Weight?

Theseus:

> Ask the sleeper.

Bacchus:

> To paint over a wound,
> To carry the sea in a net —
> Is the same as to ask a woman
> About rights and wrongs.

Theseus:

> She is the one who led out a captive...

Bacchus:

> She learned the web of feelings.
> Do not confuse her with a choice,
> You yourself answer for the maiden.

Theseus:

> What Theseus makes his own...

Bacchus:

> She will perish, wallowing in ashes.
> Between her endless beauty
> And an hour-long blossom,
>
> Between passion that maims
> And a deathless dream,
> Between a moment and eternity,
> Choose, — the choice is yours!

Yield, you who have embraced too much,
The maiden to the god.

Theseus:

She will never get past
My avid desire!

Bacchus:

My Ariadne
Will have new feelings.

Theseus:

Do you hope to stop up with wax
The splash of the reckless oar?

Bacchus:

My Ariadne
Will have new hearing.

Theseus:

A woman who has known a man at her side
Will never desire a god!

Bacchus:

My Ariadne
Will have a new sense of touch.

Theseus:

I — through the sacrificial incense!
I — in the opium of nights!

Bacchus:

My Ariadne
Will not have those eyes.

Theseus:

But don't you know that widows
In the hour of unboned caresses . . .

Bacchus:

New appearance, and new
Sight, and new step...

Theseus:

At even my most hushed call —
She's off into the night! To the chest of her past!

Bacchus:

New form, and new
Sight, and new essence...

Theseus:

With every fingernail am I inscribed
In her heart's virginal clay!

Bacchus:

The features that she cherished as a mortal
She won't recognize as a goddess.

Theseus:

Then why, double-stinged,
One night did you give the two of us?

Bacchus:

So that she might know
The difference between sky and gutter.

A woman who has known a god at her side
Will not desire the earthly.
There is no *your* Ariadne!
Go out into the palace square

Of seven-gated Thebes,
The city of new dawn,
And burn incense
To Bacchus and Ariadne!

Yield, you who have known much,
The maiden to the god.

Theseus:

Not by Gaia, not by Hera,
But by Aphrodite did I swear!

Bacchus:

You went into the Minotaur's cave
Meeker than a lamb . . .

All greatness has a price —
Spirit! — while in the flesh.
The weight of the trampled oath
Pay off with your essence.

Man, decide: the day dawns.
The twilight of dream and reality.
The sky-vault
Is filled with the flocks of morning.

                                   — Say good-bye to your wife!

Theseus:

But let me whisper at least a word to her:
She was not drawn to a coward!

Bacchus:

The hour for lovers' whisperings
Is *done*. — It is the hour of sailing.

Theseus:

But in her eyes — cisterns
Of tears in the twilight of the morning! —
I will be a traitor!

Bacchus:

Yes. As a traitor you will vanish!

Theseus:

At least in this one thing do not lie to her:
I yielded, but still loving!

Bacchus:

> So that even as a goddess
> She would not forget you?

> Hush...for all eternity.

Theseus:

> This is not within a man's limits!
> Greater than human strength
> Is this feat!

Bacchus:

> So become a deity.

Theseus:

> Not even my smallest finger will I move,
> Though I lie prostrate on the flagstones!

Bacchus:

> The Theban has
> A wondrous drink, a cure for memory:
> It changes *here* into *somewhere*,
> It changes *stay* into *sail*...

Theseus:

> Neither Hades, nor Lethe,
> For him who does not wish to forget!
> (*To Ariadne*)
> She sleeps, although poor and hard
> Her couch, — don't you want to wake up?
> Naxos: my wings' skeleton!

Bacchus:

> Island of sacrifice: Naxos.
> Go without looking back:
> So that neither step, nor sigh...

Theseus:

> There is no other Ariadne
> Except for Bacchus's.

Bacchus:

> (*in Theseus's wake*)
> God!

FIFTH TABLEAU

THE SAIL

The palace square in Athens. Morning. Aegeus, Priest, Seer.

Aegeus:

> The night is no kinder than the day,
> And the day is no kinder than the night.
> Three days for me of torment
> Now, three nights in fire

I writhe, out of my last strength
I sharpen my weak sight.
My son, who *was* —
If only I could see your ashes!

My treasure inalienable!
Better had he never been given to me!
No more do I pray — that he be alive,
No more do I pray — that he be victorious.

Just like a slave to the dipper
Clings, tarred to the groin,
His urn do I ask for, —
Gods! — pinches of dust,

Ashes…O dark cloud of wings,
Arrows over Athenian shores!
My son, who *has been*!

Seer:

Your son, who *remained*,

King! Amid the gray-streaked sea,
Amid scattered waterwhirls,
Thunderous Nereus is alive,
The defender of your flesh and bone, —

Alive still is Poseidon!
From the mound of crashing
Wave, from depth out of depth
He guards the child

Of your old age!
Do not fear the wrathful depths!
The sacrificial skiff
With the white sail will enter

The harbor. Brighter than a wing!
Into the city that has never been captive!

Aegeus:

Were that the labyrinth were
Seven hundred cubits under the foaming

Surface — oh, laughing,
I would have waited. Am I afraid of water?
But the prince of the Ocean
Is not lord of dry land.

"Safe your son sails —
White, like a wave against a cliff —

The sail." (Oh, the first upward flight
Of his oars in the hour of departure!)

"They are carrying my body —
Black, blacker than a forge
At midnight, — a rag in the wind."
The sail I foresee — black.

Black! Blacker than the wings
Of crows — over the strait!
My son, who *has been*!
In reality, in actuality, in life,

Anew! The news is bad:
The sky is bloodier than a sacrificial calf!

Seer:

Your son, who *is*,
King! In beauty and in glory!

Alive! Not burned up, but burning,
Striking — like the purple fire
Of Lemnos. Old man, he exists —
That son of yours! Not a fistful in an urn…

Twine roses around
Your brow! Not your body around an urn!
He is alive in spirit and flesh
And sails under the white

Sail.

Aegeus:

    If you are lying
It would have been better for you
Not to have been born into this world! You will rot like a dog!

Priest:

King, do not anger the prophet.

Easier it would be for a builder
Not to know the cracks and splits
In his own home than for this old man

To speak falsehood looking at the entrails
Of the sacrifices. Quit your anger and praise Zeus.

Seer:

The mind — that is real,
The flesh — that is a veil.

If you want an object
To speak, reduce yourself to ash…

Aegeus:

Is he alive, his hand warm?

Seer:

Bread from the embers is not warmer.

Aegeus:

But is he unharmed? Is he
Sound? Is he flushed…

Seer:

In its shell the seed
Of a pearl is not safer
At the lowest depth of the abyss.
He is safe as fleshless spirit.

Aegeus:

Not mutilated, not…
So my line will not dry up?

Whom did I mourn in song?
Into the harbor — instead of a cave!
But he is not safe and dishonored?

Seer:

By magic is he safe — and faith.

Aegeus:

Magic?

Seer:

It is not for us to know:
But know that he went beloved by someone.
By faith — in the body, which is straight,
And into heaven, which is full.

On fire with magic and faith
And by them commanded…
But having honed his blow,
Old man — yet another victory!

Darkening with purple
His sword — he smiled, as if
A god. Without lifting the sword,
Old man, the victory is heavier.

He came out exhausted
But bright.

Aegeus:

Glory! But what was the
Monster? A serpent or a boar?

Seer:

That boar is called

Passion of the flesh. *It* has he slain,
Moved by a higher passion.

Aegeus:

Wind, do not spare the sails!
My longed-for son, hasten on!
(*To the Priest and the Seer*)
Friends, let us hasten to meet them!
Do not betray me, old age!
Enter Messenger.

Messenger:

King, in the gray of the deep
A black sail has been spotted.

Aegeus:

Death!
(*to the Seer*)
       I will repay you, liar,
Not with earthly, but with other, coin!
Priest, report to the gods:
Going to meet his son

The king vanished.
       (*Aegeus disappears. The messenger follows him. From the other side
       of the square the citizens are filing in, unnoticed by the departing men.*)

Chorus of Citizens:

Woe! Woe!
A sharp blade!
Sea, sea,
What do you carry?
In your overflowing sumptuous coffer —
Sea, sea, what do you bring us?
Roses, roses for our temples?[21]
Tears, tears for our eyes?

Woe! Woe!
A cruel serpent!
From your cupped hands of blue
Your largesse — what will we receive,
Sea, sea? Let it be blue,
The wave, or gone gray like an old man —
Only may the sail come out white!

Woe! Woe!
A bent sickle!
Sea, sea,
Double-hearted
Is your temper: after raging
Like a boar of the overgrown forest, you will rest
Like a white lamb, parting its curls.
Sea: a furious tub!

Fate, fate,
A covered vessel!
Sea, sea,
What will you reveal
To the eyes? Behind the white paling
Of foam — what? What gift
For Athens? A shredded cloth?
Fate: a covered washtub!

Fate, Fate,
A silent weaver!
Sea, sea,
Above the masts
Is your wave! With his fist clenched
Lord Poseidon strikes
All his subjects under the depths.
Fate: a closed palm!

Fate, Fate,
It will go on — how long?
Sea, sea,
All the salt
Of your depths and all your boil
Of foam we will drink up,
We will eat up like bread: boiling tar,
Fate: a cruel valley!

Fate, Fate . . .
Where is freedom?
Sea, sea,
What is in the skiff?
Did Crete return our first-borns,
Or the brotherly urn:
The ashes of seven springs and — the smoke
Of seven youths along with the eighth.

Fate, Fate,
Hidden timber!
Sea, sea,
Beneath the grass
Is your wave! It has broken up into brooks.
Sea! Sea! What is that sail
There, like a crow amid the canvas?
Woe! Woe! It is black!

Messenger:
No more is —
The King. Overfull

Is the goblet of grief and gloom.
Into the seething of the waves
Fell the king from the cliff.

Having seen his calamity
From afar, from on high,
He fell — to meet his son
From a steep cliff, three hundred cubits.

In his fever of fatherly love,
In his ashes of vanity,
Into the four-hundred-cubit depth,
From the three-hundred-cubit height.

Not the fast-flying eagle,
King of wings and talons —
Merely an old man from three hundred
Granite cubits.

Like the fierce gyrfalcon —
Into the foaming wool of the waves,
He shot upwards — the first to meet
His son's dust.

Not in the angry quarrel
Of winds and sails —
Not in the sea, but in grief,
Did he drown himself!

In the foam of his own lips,
Their bloody rim,
In the eternity of his own shadow,
In the depths of his own darkness,

In the brief, killing
Word: why?
In his bottomless basin
Of fatherly love.

Where the precipice is like a wedge,
Where the foam roars —
The maelstrom received
Him as he flew into its bosom.

Chorus of Citizens:
Woe! Woe! From the red cliffs —
Woe! Woe! Like a rock he fell,

Our king. Flood the square,
You fatherless and sonless,

Flock without a shepherd!
Woe! Woe! Without a king!

Woe! Woe! Twice he fell!
The roaring green-curled wave
Snatched the old man.
The young one was flung
By his blind daring
Into the monster's jaws.
Woe! Woe! And black — the rigging!

For the kites — a bloody feast!
Woe! Woe! Twice orphaned
Is our land, crumbled to pieces.
Instead of sumptuous pastures —
The kites' bloody gathering...
Woe! Woe! A sea of tears!

Woe! Woe! Blood of our blood!
Childless mother, prepare
The black attire of grief!
Stark — across the sea's expanse —
The fluttering sleeve of grief.
Oh, it is not black, but bloody!

Right he was, to have launched
Himself from the cliffs!
Better it would be into this life —
In which justice is not expected —
Not to give birth and not to be born,
And not to know, how fresh the wind is...
Woe! Woe! Woe!
(Theseus enters accompanied by the maidens and youths.)

Theseus:
                              But where
Are the laurels for the victor?
Here am I, alive and invincible!
As if on tapestries
Your leader flew over sea-boulders,

With auspicious news:
It is this: with a full count of seven
Maidens, with seven youths
Together — I return to my native roof.

They are safe and unscathed —
Like the trees in spring!
Seven hoped for and seven
Awaited; I — the eighth.

ARIADNE

Fallen is the Minotaur, and the wave
Carried us away! Into a bloody mound
Is he fallen! And with the Minotaur — Minos.
But why this reception?

Why are the sheep under cover?
Why the women hiding?
I don't hear greetings!
Does the sea muffle them?

Why are you like fish in the foam?
Why are you like lizards in the grass?
Are you mute from joy?
Or am I myself deaf?

Are you blind from joy?
For here it is, in front of you,
The beauty and stronghold
Of Athens. Or should I

Go back? Once more the sea
Disturbing with my keel?
Only I echo myself
In this thunderous

Silence. Not greeted,
No eyes' glance!
So here it is, the meeting,
So here it is, the honor,

So here they are, the handfuls
Of roses, the laurels of peaks
For the warrior-bullfighter
From Athens the free!

In the hour of grief and sighs
Swift was my steel.
In response to the clamor of my deeds,
Are you mute, O city?

The deed of my hands —
Already the news of the bull
Has thundered all through the world! —
But here — not even a branch in my hand?!

Hearts without feeling!
Bodies without hearts!

But — worst wonder of all:
That — even my father —

Did not come out to meet me,
To rest all his burden
On the might of my muscles. . .
Or am I indeed fatherless?

Athenians, I am burning!
My forehead is clamped in a vise!
Tell Aegeus
That his son...

Seer:
                    Dead
Is the King. Not to be born —
That, in this kingdom of vanities,
Is the bedrock.

Theseus:
                  The murderer
Of his majesty?

Seer:
                You.

"If the bull is slain of the two of us,
White, whiter than steam
The sail." Thus into fatherly ears
Fell your word.

"If black ashes cover me —
Black, blacker than tarry pitch expect
The sails." With what magic word
Is your mind spellbound?

What is that serpent
Under your root?

Theseus:
Widowed of a wondrous maiden,
Exhausted with sorrow —

I sailed. When the world is no longer dear,
Black is dear to the eye.
That is why I forgot
To change the sail.

Chorus of Youths:
In the hour of leaf-shedding springs,
Of wounds, unknown to doctors,
Black, only the color black
Is tolerable for grieving eyes.

54

ARIADNE

In the hour of gaping fissures
— Ah! — and all hopes have given up! —
Black, black to the eye — is green,
Black, black to the eye — is fresh.

Who will dare to set out in a ship
Like a sprightly white-fleeced lamb,
If in his breast, as in an urn,
Our leader carries a dead maiden?

In the hour when he lost everything,
In the hour when he buried all,
Black, black to the eye — is beautiful,
Black, black to the eye — is dear.

Darkness is breath without inhaling!
Darkness is the touch of a veil!
As the tired warrior — for a ravine,
The eye yearns for blackness.

In the hour of broken embraces,
— Ah, my bride, lie with somebody else! —
Black, black to the eye is — distinct,
Black, black to the eye is — welcome.

In the hour of abandoned shores,
— Of wounds unknown to doctors, —
Black, black is the only color
That does not slice at weeping eyes.

In the hour when he did not notice roses,
In the hour when his heart grew gray,
Black, black to the eye — is bright,
Black, black to the eye — is white.

That is why under that malicious
Sign — the sailors sailed.
Of whitest Ariadne
We are all black widowers.

We all are black Nubians
Of sorrow — chopped-down oaks!
We all are murderers of Aegeus,
And on all of us is the accursed sign —
Black...

Seer:

I swear by midday magic,
There is in it the chisel of divine power!

55

My son, whom of the fatal gods
Did you anger?

Man, even when hitting, is good-natured,
A god strikes in the back.
Whose fealty did you break,
Son, of the immortal powers?

Against which unseen being
Have you shown yourself unjust?
From which of the Olympian heights
Did you throw down thunder?

Son, you are punished
By an unearthly law, — by a finger struck down!
Whose jealousy, of the Olympian women,
Did you provoke?

You are but a dried-out splinter,
Man, and they lay hands on you!
The mind can conceive nothing
More vengeful than the Olympian goddesses.

They will exact the penalty, you shard of pottery,
You spilled vessel!
My son, for whom of the fatal ones
Are you guilty?

Priest:

                          They carry
The body. Wound around with seaweed.

Theseus:

I recognize you, Aphrodite!

Prague, October 1924.

PHAEDRA

Lovesick Phaedra. Apulian Red Figure calyx krater , ca 350 BC. (British Museum, London. F272)

PHAEDRA

CHARACTERS:
Phaedra
Theseus
Hippolytus
Nurse
Manservant
Friends (male)
Womenservants

FIRST TABLEAU

HALT

Forest. HIPPOLYTUS in a circle of friends.

Chorus of youths
O, thicket! O, call!
O, new hills'
Heights!
Let us glorify the chase!
What is better than fighting?
Hunting![1]

Praise to Artemis for heat, for sweat,
For the black thicket — brighter is
Hades' entrance! — for leaves, for pine needles,
For hot hands in the play of the brook, —
Praise to Artemis for everything and all things
Of the forest.

Ambush. Alarm:
What — horn or bough?
Branching
Bush — or deer?
No, the rushing shadow
Of Callisto![2]

Praise to Artemis for ford, for bank,
For — unto gasping swift run
Along leafy ravine.
As a springtime watercourse you sound!
Praise to Artemis for senses' and muscles'
Joy.

A branch caught in the eyes.
What — stump or boar?
Snaky
Lump? A braid of root?
With a beast's leap —
Into the valley!

Praise to Artemis for the gaze, for hearing,
Without touching it, the fluff you will not blow away
From the stamen. O scent: O sight
Of thickets! — Burning lips in the play of the brook...
A deer you become, bounding after
A deer!

Forehead streams, mouth dry.
In the instructive scent —
Of moss, of fur
Breath, of horn and of moss
Breath. Chest — like a bellows.
— Ho! — Echo!

Praise to Artemis for shame, for harm,
For false joy, for false tracks,
False move, — all torments in vain!
Hidden supper and night in a ditch!
Praise to Artemis for all the play
Of the forest.

Chase ended. Fire abated.
Coolness. Halt.
Checking
Chest, flank, to blood beaten,
The hunter disembowels
The beast.

Praise to Artemis for horn, for tusk,
The latest boldness, the latest cry
Of the hunter, — moaned, sighed
Has the forest. It has turned over. Roots ground to dust!
Praise to Artemis for fur, for...
Flies'

Buzz. Breath gone.

We have no need of marrying!
Both now and in the future
We glorify friendship!
We glorify manliness!
For wives there is no delight in us!

Not for us to cherish offspring.
We glorify brotherhood!
We glorify virginity!
House with householdful?
No, forest with the unforeseen!
Wild game we will be called,
The army of Artemis.
Like a deer you prick up your ears,
You do not disturb the earth!
We glorify swift-run,
We glorify swift-breath!
Do not crow, that you are straight!
They bend — the tender-lipped!
To fall in love is to bow:
We sing lovelessness!
A different deliciousness —
In burning resin.
To take a wife is to weep,
We sing weddinglessness!

Forest, forest-greenness!
Swift streamlet!
An archer is no lodger:
To wive is to settle down!
Neither troubles, nor delights —
Quiet murder.
A proud man is no father:
To multiply is to divide oneself!

Not yet given — already taken away!
Short, short, the life of the hunter.
For a moment — flowers flowered for him.
More short-lived than an arrow!
Water flows, woes pile up.
They hunt for the hunter:
Night, road, stone, sleep —
All, and hidden in all
The gods. Not to the vain-wise priest
Is divinity drawn — to daring.
The brave man does not live long.
He himself is marked prey.
Not to high-flown intentions
Is divinity drawn — to youth.
Marble has a weakness for sunburn.
Each youth is a bread-gift
Of a god. More fervently than a dancing girl
Is divinity drawn to the perishable.
More than we have need —
Of them, we — to the marble ones are necessary.

There it is, the forest! There it is, the bow!
Because of their cavemen's rudeness
Of all Artemis's servants
Not one falls in love.
There it is, life! There it is, gold!
Because of their far clearsightedness
Of all Artemis's children
Not one wives!

And ever and now
On hills and in gully,
Let us sing the goddess,
The only friend
Of our fate and of our daring —
Artemis green-curled!

And loudly and much,
Both in fables and in masks,[3]
The sunrising god's
Twin[4] let us sing:
Man-equal, majestic
Artemis wide-striding.

More eternal than water mills
More eternal than flour mills
Like laurel ever-green
Like Pontus[5] ever-waving —
So eternal in our heart of clay
Artemis proud-necked.

A hundred have I taken, in this I crashed down.
In the hour of the breaking of ribs,
As long as we have even a sigh in us —
Let us sing, let us sing
The other-than-woman, the hidden
Artemis man-haughty.

Let us praise her — and louder!
With darkness and dawn,
There she is with hound,
There she is with doe,
Amid leaves, as amid flocks,
Night and day,
With a not-reaching-her-knee
Tunic — bracelet! — fillet! — comb! —
In a run that outstrips the body.

Along labyrinths
Of hazy greenery

61

There she is with the faithful
Nymph, Callisto,
Not cooling
In ardor and in rosy glow,
With a shadow that
Cannot keep up with her movement,
Lost in the breaks of her
Run. Leading without those led.

Can full happiness
Be seen as a whole?
There she is in the thicket,
There she is in her own
Heart. Fall in,
Forest motley-floored!
So that with boles like a paling
She be encircled — bind yourselves together, walls! —
To a watercourse she has handed over
Exhausted limbs...

Time, give in, and foam, vanish!
The tunic will not catch up with the knees.
Disgraced one, sit upon a stump.
The shadow will not catch up with the movement.
Against time we will bend:
The breast will not catch up with the breath.
Against time we will drive:
The lock of hair will not catch up with the nape,
The ear — with the echo, the poet — with life...
But Artemis's run will catch up with
The deer.

Amid grasses and amid leaves — glorify her!
Thick leaves — her curls.
Amid branchlets and amid twigs — glorify her!
Branches? no, her arms, legs.
All that tries to get out of the circle[6] is hers!
In every strain — her muscles!
Friends, even on turf honor her!
Black roots — her will.
Unshakeable her heart —
Bare rock-blocks — her heart!

Beast howling, forest blowing,
Both apart and together
Let us sing the lily
Of the white garments not once
Darkened with love's filth:
Artemis stone-hearted.

At the needful moment — strike us,
Arrow without heirs!
Let us sing innocence,
Let us sing haughtiness
Of flesh known only to a lake!
Artemis quivering-nostrilled.

But a wonder — through the leaves!
But a wonder — as in a puff of smoke...
And in our songs and in our thoughts
We fix next to the
Man-terrible goddess —
Hippolytus deer-eyed

With a languor-resistant mouth
With a mouth — like a bow not brittle!
The goddess's friend
Let us sing. Let us sing
The lofty friend of Artemis —
Hippolytus set-against-women.

His nose — has scented the keen,
His forehead — has moved the difficult.
Aegeus's grandson,
Theseus's son,
Despiser of the feminine clan —
Hippolytus of Troezen we sing.

We will drive storm clouds, we will bring together cups,
We will sink ourselves in glorification
Of the unsociable favorite
Of the chaste goddess.
Of the unsociable one her beloved —
Of Hippolytus the uncatchable —

Wondrous whose hearing, marvelous whose gaze.
Under bush, where sleep overwhelms,
Who the keenest of all, who the best-looking of all?
Hippolytus! Hippolytus!
Yet still tribute no one has levied —
From Hippolytus the uncatchable.

Boars, bristle up! does, lament!
Noted for his eye-measuring —
Who the most accurate of all, who the most skilled of all?
Hippolytus! Hippolytus!
A lighter leap no one has had —
Than Hippolytus insurpassable.

On fire our bush-trailblazer!
Take a look, in the hours of prayers,
Who the most steadfast of all, who the most ardent of all?
Hippolytus! Hippolytus!
Never shamed the name —
Of Hippolytus the tireless.

Women have arisen, sun is out,
Encircled, woman-surrounded —
Who the most feral of all, who the quietest of all?
Hippolytus! Hippolytus!
No one has passed him in recklessness —
Hippolytus the implacable.

A wild boar at one sitting.
For the grape sweat thirsts.
Hippolytus alone does not eat,
Hippolytus alone does not drink.
Why, having crowned the chase,
Marvel-boar having laid low,
Hippolytus alone is stern?
Hippolytus alone is fastidious?
A maiden perhaps met him in the forest?
A doe for a maiden a lion took?
Or — a boar for a fox —
Takes us for maidens?
Fat and juices — pour and cut!
Time is dear — drink and stand!
Woman-fighter, drink and eat!
Boar-beater, drink and glorify
With us rushing — rushed —
Youth unreturning!
Intoxicated grape.
Boar's being gobbled up.
Is youth long?
Remember!

Hippolytus:

Boar gladdens not,
Forest gladdens not,
Life gladdens not.
A dream I
Have dreamed. Darkening for me all existing
Women — my mother visited my
Dream. The lady who lives
In me alone
Visited her house.
Here — the urn of her ashes!
Her only home on earth.
I had not noticed, but the night glowed,

64

As she arrived and as she entered.
I will go gray, I will say, as now:
No entrance was there, there was: "here!
I am!" Like a boat from behind the waves,
An apparition from the earth —
Flagstones — days — prohibitions — through.
No face was there. There was the eyes'
Gaze. Not stars and not rays,
Of the whole body and of the whole soul
Gaze, — so, a doe's on her fawns
Gaze, so — as mothers look who are
Dead.
          As if in the edge of a mirror
The gaze a figure grew.
Thrown stone's circles!
Bridge of the nose. In two arches
The even brows. Under the lips
A will of stone — like an arch.
With a puff of lips: — Speak!
No speech was there. There was a hand's
Sign. Silence-filled thunder.
There was of the waxen hand — a relentless
Raising. Her shroud gaped.
For her son — a finger pointing to a wound!
It melted. It began to float.
Dear friends, how
The breast and the wound to see at once?!
No speech was there. Blood flowed
To the ground, onto my hands, — without strength
Was I prostrated — still the finger floated
Higher, higher it soared — until,
Having stopped, did it not seal the mouth —
Against maternal words? Against mine?
Further there was nothing. There was — smoke
There...In the circle of ten fingers
No flesh was there. There was a shroud,
Steam. Steam I grasp! Simple. Empty.
Steam's melting under a hoping
Hand...

Friends:
                    Dream!
Hippolytus:
          A knowing...[7]
Friends:
                    Delirium!
          — By a daydream confused!

— By a thought stung!
— Are spells few?
— Fables we do not heed!
— Just — steam!
— Just — smoke
Of the mind — In us —
Essence. What is not us —
Mirage. — The evil eye!
— Full moon's
Eye. — Moon arrows'
Poison. — Dear our friend!
Too much have you eaten!
— Too much have you drunk
With evening. Furious is
Bacchus in the hour of play.
Not even moon
Vapor — wine
Vapors. Fumes!
Brain-bent tipsiness!
— The dead sleep!
— But mortals drink!
(In chorus.)
In spite of deliria and in spite of spells —
Drink and laugh, while you're not bald!

Manservant:

A mother from the grave does not rise in vain:
My lord, beware!
Appearance of PHAEDRA.

Phaedra:

To the noble archers — greeting.
In the wild brake walking and walking
Imperceptibly — from glade to glade —
All womenservants being lost,
I look for the way of return.
Show me the way and the slope —
Back. From this faith-breaking thicket
Where is the road, leading to Troezen?
You will not repent, having served
Me.

Hippolytus:

High lady!
In a place of head-spinning terrors,
On the heights, nothing will serve,
Except — are they of woman? — *to be able* and *to dare.*
Together with good advice: in future
Keep not to bushes, but to a distaff —
There is a support for you along unsteady
Paths, murderous for the feet
Of a woman.

(To the servant.)
> You who know, lead down
The lady.
Phaedra:
> About one thing permit me
> To know: what do you in the valley's peace?
> For — kingly features!
Hippolytus:
> Artemis I serve. And you?
> By your speech — an outlander?
Phaedra:
> Aphrodite I serve — I am a Cretan.

SECOND TABLEAU

INTERROGATION

A sick PHAEDRA in the circle of her servants.

One of the womenservants:
> I pick out the step of the Nurse.
Nurse:
> *(entering)*
> She sleeps?
Womenservants:
> *(one after another)*
>   — As if she had forgotten herself.
> — The illness is unknown. — From across the sea.
> She didn't sleep. — But she hasn't been awake either.
> She will begin to speak — of odd things.
> You give her something hot — she wants something cold.
> You cool it — she wants something hot.
> Steam — she turns her little head away.
> — The same with her clothes — you wear yourself out!
> Like this — you freeze me, like that — you smother me.
> Again — pull on, again — pull off!
> She looks at the fire — "oh, the house burns!"
> You screen her — "oh, dark as a well!"
> Light — her eyes hurt, darkness — she's frightened.
> — But such eyes — no to that tale!
> More than the little hands are the little eyes pitiful.
> Two hands wring and twist —
> More than the little eyes are the little hands pitiful.
> Again wrings out, again squeezes!
> Now you begin whispering: "Ah, am I near death?"
> At the sound of voices — palms to her ears.
> No longer her own, no longer herself.

Always, with horses and overgrown places,
Delirium.

Nurse: Know the illness — know the cure.
But without finding out — no healing.
Rootlet-I'll-bring-leaflet,
Three hills, searching, I went through.

Servants:
Always a swift horse she asks for.
Blazes, blazes the fire from her cheeks!
And she tears the bracelets from her arms so!

Phaedra:
I hear, I hear a horse's galloping!

Nurse:
Your own heart's beat.

Sleep, milk mine, sleep, my all!
From Athens she smiled happy
With praises and with raptures,
The sailors she urged on, —
The sailing ship almost took a wave!
She caught sight of the forest: "Oh, thickets!"
Leaps of a goat, bounds of a hare!
Among the bushes after her chasing,
We were breathless, run off our legs.
Not her own did she return from the forest.

Phaedra:
I tell you: high
The green myrtle bough.
I hear, I hear a horse's galloping!

Nurse:
Your own heart's beat.

To question deeply, I have not the boldness:
What in the dense forest was met?
Perhaps wicked people?
Her little necklace is intact.
Perhaps a forest beast, a beast with fangs —
Her little dress would be in rags.
Nothing — a ring? they would have found it! —
In the forest dark she did not leave anything,
Except her rosy cheeks. Her soul only.

Womenservants:
Of forest whispers she has heard enough,
Of leafy green trifles.
— But I think, she ate too much fruit,
Not prescribed by the sciences.
— But I think, she smelled too many flowers

Fever-making, unknown.
  — But I think — she is weary without the lips
Of the king.

Phaedra:
                    Like a hammer into my temple!
Like boiling water it runs along my cheeks!
Cool the boiling water!
Stop the hammer!

Womenservants:
And always she tosses! Always she torments herself!
And a shirt against fate
You will not cut — cut it out as you will.
It is high time for the arrival
Of the king. Poor soul: everywhere hurts!
The king she calls, the king she demands.
He comes, he will be here — merciful gods! —
The king from across the sea.

Phaedra:
                         No, from the forest.
Nearer, nearer, the horse's galloping!
Lower, lower, the terrible bough!
Crack, skin! Flow, juice!

Nurse:
Your hexed heart's beat.

Your horse, poor girl, is between your
Ribs. It seems, in an ill hour we left
Athens. To Troezen, where three woes
We have, — it seems, in an ill hour we arrived.
To others' gods even with incense
You cannot reach. Toward others' gods
Our foreheads, toward our own our backs —
What necessity for us — to be in Troezen? Sonny[8] to Athens
For a blessed, long guesting
He would have called. Here three woes, there half-woe.
Even if it were not chicken's milk[9]
  — Those were our usual gods.

Phaedra:
In the forest a high bough,
On the bough a heavy fruit.
Throbs the fruit, bends the bough.

Nurse:
Your hexed heart's pace.

Womenservants:
An ailment from across the sea.

Nurse:
                      From the wood.

Bough and galloping in her mind. It would not snap
The bough. But what fruit? Of your own thoughts
The fruit. But what galloping? But there isn't any at all.

Phaedra:

You will fly at full gallop,
I will bow to you from the bough.
Heavy the fruit for that bough.
Heavy the fruit for the bough — anguish.

Nurse:

In your own brain the splinter —
The bough. Blood with reason has squabbled —
Half with half.
The tree-trunk with the sick core.
Old the song, old the tale…

One of the womenservants:

Should we not notify the stepson?

Others:

— Painfully severe!
— Stingy with his heart!

Phaedra:

Ended the galloping!
Snapped the bough!

Why around me — such things
Do I see? Where am I? Who am I? What am I?
Why on all — such a
Spell? Who am I? What am I? Whose am I?
Why is my hair loose?

Nurse:

Sleep didn't come — it untwisted itself.

Phaedra:

Why am I half-dressed?

Nurse:

No hump — no shame.

Phaedra:

But you lack looks,
Little sisters!

Womenservants:

The whole night we shook
Over you, beauty, trembling
For your life, — the whole night you shook!

Phaedra:

Fever is talkative —
I didn't say anything?

Nurse:

Not a few nothings.

Phaedra:

I did not call anyone?

(To the Womenservants:)
    Since when are magpies mute?
Womenservants:
    You talked, but unknowable…
    Dark the thought, dark the pit…
    You called, but an unknown.
    Water flows, just try to weigh it!
    And it's unknown who, unknown what…
    Some new illness.
Nurse:
                    No, an ancient one.
    Earlier than we and you. We are of two days —
    We. With kings it does not change itself.
    Earlier than life it begins.
    An ancestral, not an orphan,
    Grief, without it, the whole race of people
    Would have died out, in one hour — all completely!
    It never would have even begun…
    If a certain force had not burst forth
    From heaven.
    (to the Womenservants:)
                    However, it's early for you
    To know. Go for a walk, while yet foolish!
    I instead will tuck the queen into bed.
    Lullaby-reckoning
    Sea-bottom-cockle-shell.
    Like that, little baby?
Phaedra:
    Like that, little mother.
    Womenservants exit.
Nurse:
    From afar, from long ago I will take things up:
    Bitter women in your line, —
    And such will be your fame in the future!
    Pasiphae loved a monster:[10]
    The king ceased to please, the beast was dear.
    Her daughter are you or not her daughter?
    Maternal blood-drop of evil!
    Your present spouse sold Ariadne
    To the god in the hour of sleep.
    To Ariadne — a sister
    Twice: by womb and by marriage bed.
    Only, with the god there was no dealing:
    The god did not please, dust was dear:
    Passion was there, but terror here.
Phaedra:
    With a god-equal sister
    For me to compare myself is difficult.

Nurse: Children of one mother
Wives of one husband —
Pasiphae's bitter daughters.
Ariadne and your husband year-siblings[11]
Were. She would be — ay, do I lie? —
And so? — How old is the king? —
If the god had not taken her to the middle of heaven…

Phaedra:
Obviously, more than forty.

Nurse:

A lot more than forty.
He's almost worth fifty.
Yet with this king — by his face an old man! —
Don't blush, don't butter up, —
Phaedra — are you indeed happy?

Phaedra:
The shepherd can be without a sheep,
What without the shepherd — the sheep?

Nurse:
Phaedra, he could be your father!
A stepfather named himself your husband!

Phaedra:
Without ivy the oak grows stronger:
Death — to the stalk of ivy!

Nurse:
Phaedra, he is not beloved by you!

Phaedra:
Nana, I love him.

Nurse:
Here is she who nursed, here is she who raised
You! A beauty — a find[12] — an old man
Loves. Wilderness[13] for my ears, outlandishness!

Phaedra:
Is he husband to me or no husband?

Nurse:
Break, my aching bones!
Husband, beauty, yet not to you alone:
Ariadne's — fold your fingers into your palm[14] —
Antiope's,[15] now
Phaedra's, and tomorrow…Here is she who nursed
You! The black blood of Pasiphae
Unrepentant — into water
Is turned! Your own
Husband, you think? No, inherited.
What sort of joy — well and good with a sister's
Husband, Phaedra, but this — widower!
Each and all say:

72

With the inconsolable widower of a goddess!
For, Phaedra, *hers* he is up to now,
Ariadne's. Anew the master
Ask — always widowed.

With the dove in the deep forest
He would not set you, if you were needed.
Phaedra, he to you is no husband!

Phaedra:

Nana, to him am I wife.
And stop your stupid talk!

Nurse:

Amazing to me is your "I love!"
And the womanservant defends the hearth.
What — "I love?" There — *how*
You love! For ten years of wedlock
It is clear: in what way, why, for what
You love. Well, then?

Phaedra:

In the first place — he's brave.

Nurse:

Birds without wings, fish without gills —
There is no husband without bravery.
Further?

Phaedra:

With every passerby simply[16]
He speaks.

Nurse:

Talkative? Who knows with whom!
In the second place. Next,
In the third place?

Phaedra:

Generous.

Nurse:

Not a spouse — a treasure!
Brave, good, you say — and what else?
The same thing lies nearby, heh-heh!
Only a wee bit younger.
Further?

Phaedra:

He honors he who is far.[17] But little does it
Matter, for what, why!

Nurse:

Grind
More finely! Power and simplicity — are poverty
For love. Still
What, for what?

Phaedra: Is not the gray hair of Theseus

Wise?
Nurse: I say, sift
More often! Your sieve is trash!
Wise — and what
Else?
Phaedra:
                  Upon the vanquished with mildness
He looks.
Nurse:
                  And there is nothing else?
Phaedra:
                              Simply:
Husband to me.
Nurse:
                  A glorious — word — your mouth
Wrung out…All —
Perhaps? The nightingale should always trill
In the little garden! But now — there is nothing
Else? — So *I* will speak. My blow
Against Theseus: he's old.
With a spider, Phaedra, have they mated you!
Whatever you've taken into your head, whatever you…On an old man
Take vengeance. You are not sinful in anything with regard to him.
Into your husband's house you entered
As the latest wife, the third wife.
Two wives met a young one
On the threshold. Not of this earth
Wives — into the house they led
The young woman. "Live," they said, "Be joyful."
Two wives the young woman by the hand
Lead, your nights and days,
Phaedra, in their shadow,
But the dark bedchamber — their cloud.
Two wives to you, the third, behind their hand
Whisper. Dishes from hands fly, —
The Amazon's glance is
Sharp, — and do not look behind the curtain!
The whole court, the whole house with their eyes
Looks. The fire in the hearth has died away —
Ariadne's sigh.
Cruel their heart, sacred their place!
Two wives the young woman marry off to
The Styx.[18] You carry a cup to your lips —
Ariadne's heavy
Ladle…Clusters of grapes?

Antiope's, Ariadne's,
Tears. You carry a cup from your lips, —
The Amazon's taste is
Bitter, — as is that of the mouth of Theseus.
The embittered one — what did you do —
When you took him? Oil in the nightlamp is dried up —
Ariadne's secret
Sign. Suffocating walls, musty.
Two wives cursed the young
Womb. You rise from the couch the same woman
As when you lay down:
A meager wife, a useless wife.[19]
Two snakes put the evil eye on the birthing
Bed…Laughter in the house does not ring —
Ariadne's sob
For a child — who would be more beloved than her soul!
Two wives, do I say? no, two snakes,
Phaedra! Your belt up to now has not been taut[20] —
Deed of the Amazon's
Hands. On a marshy bank
You established yourself! With the cooling impression,
Freezing — of their shoulders, of their hips
The bridal couch
Is bespelled. — Do not hide in your little palms!
Lechery, not marriage, I say, without a youngling!

Phaedra:

If there were — I would rejoice. There are none —
I do not grieve.

Nurse:

                  He who does not
Give pleasures — neither of them, nor of a little babe
Is worthy. *Loving*, be fruitful —
There is the law for you and all measure.
Mother indeed honors father —
It is little — for a beautiful generation!
A wife useless and vain…

Phaedra:

I have heard! And I ask…

Nurse:

                — You are right!
Already for a while it is time
For me — to hear. As if it were stolen —
You love your husband, whence then the hollows
In your cheeks?

Phaedra:

        From this…

Nurse:

            Lie!

From this: you lie
To me, to yourself, to him, and to people.
I nursed you at my breast.
Between us speech is unnecessary:
I know, I feel, I see, I hear
All — the whole deposit[21] of all your troubles! —
That is five times what you know,
You feel, you see, you hear, you want
To know.

Phaedra:

         Like a worm, old woman, do you eat away.

Nurse:

You want, you thirst, you dare, you can
Know.

Phaedra:

         Alive, old woman, do you gnaw me.

Nurse:

I am worn out
With waiting. — Tell! — Tell all!
Always nurse
I, always nursling —

You…Of a word, what is hard is the first
Syllable! Between your mouth and this
Breast, between the breast — generous — poor —
And the lips — nowhere for a secret —
Where would it be? Between breast and lips.
For nursed passions
The breast of the nurse quivers.
Secrets, sorrows, troubles — from your shoulders
Throw them! To me — on the heart! All sadnesses!
This breast does not know overloads.

Without twisting
Paths, cloying oaths —
Always the nurse
I, always the nursling —

You! After all, mother to you, after all, daughter to me!
Besides the bloody — a milky
Voice — let's bow down to milk! —
Is: second motherhood.
Two, over a person's life,
Fates: blood's voice, milk's
Voice. Spurting from the heart
Motherhood, daughterhood
Of the drinking lips. Poison flows in veins —
I — in answer, I — nourished you.

Strong as the grave is the
Bond. — Those *days* where are they?
Always the nurse
I, always the nursling —

You. Night is poor for everything, not for thought.
On my wisdom feed,
As then — grace of those hours! —
You fed on my milk,
Whiter than Aphrodite's
Foam. — By my youth!
You weave a web, visible to me only.

Phaedra:

Frivolousness, old woman, do you babble!

Nurse:

You see dreams — perhaps already seen in your family?[22]

Phaedra:

Slander, old woman, do you sow!

Nurse:

Are they not mine, beauty,
The sins you commit?
All — the nurse's!
You? Nursling

Only. Ask the doctor about an ulcer:
He cuts cleanly — he cuts at once.
Ask the butcher about the block:
He chops cleanly — he chops with one stroke.
Not on the king, queen, do you dote!

Phaedra:

Nana, you cut on the quick!

Nurse:

Not the king, queen, do you love!

Phaedra:

Nana, you chop on the quick!
By all my torments —
Nana, truce!

Nurse:

                    Phaedra, the name!
I have exhausted the words
Of my prayers.
No nurse —
I, no nursling —
Have I. In vain my milk: gushed to the earth!
...Or is he of race so base,
That to name — it'd be easier to lift one thousand pounds?[23]

Phaedra:

He of low race? No, of high,
The highest.

Nurse:

> Hmm. Or has he bedsores?
> People go to battle, he with a woman lies,
> Some kind of drunkard without a belt?

Phaedra:

> Young enough — to marry, good enough — to rely upon.
> If they trumpet to war — first displays
> His chest.

Nurse:

> No coward, you say — it would be a real shame!
> And no slave, you say: no bull from the slaughterhouse
> Dries up your brain — So some god or other?
> Whoever he is — no evil, no fear is there,
> If he is not to you a blood son.

Phaedra:

> Stepson.
> King's son. — The end. — No secret.
> Only do not give me the name…
> That sound I cannot bear!

Nurse:

> Its letters I will not utter.
>
> From the most faithful of nurses,
> Dear one, what did you hide?
> Wonderful, wonderful this union!

Phaedra:

> From my own self I hide.

Nurse:

> By the envy of the heaven-dwellers,
> To the dear one — is it long since you confessed yourself?

Phaedra:

> Once burning tinder has been laid,
> Together with Phaedra will the secret
> Go up in flames.

Nurse:

> Shield yourself with your little hand!

Phaedra:

> Shame, of which I do not think!
> If from only words — my brow
> With blood floods…

Nurse:

> What
> Simpler? Seize the hour, which darkens all:
> Forehead — and shame on it, the hour — into thicket,
> Brake. You are not the first
> To conceal yourself with the night undergrowth…

Phaedra:

> I — with him?
> In the thickets?

Nurse:

                        The road I will tell, of all the closest.

Phaedra:

Road, which I do not see!
Step — and black circles,
Step — and like the dead.

Nurse:

                           Be up to it,
Be equal to it! The hour seize, quietest of all…

Phaedra:

A sound, which I do not hear!
A sound, unthinkable from lips
Pure.

Nurse:

           You love — few pure
Feelings. Seize the hour, the most silent of all…

Phaedra:

Delirium, do not listen to it,
Heart!

Nurse:

          Experienced, more than we
Knowing, the latest of all — our
Hour! The only hour which does not lie
Of the twenty-four. Seize a bush, densest of all,
A slope, sleepiest of all…

Phaedra:

               The grass,
The leaf will not endure it!

Nurse:

               New are you
To this deed! You will improve! Yes, a darling
Boy! Breath take, of all the deepest:
Level-like-a-full-spoon —
Breath.

Phaedra:

         But I do not breathe at all!
No strength! No veins! No arms! No legs!
Mouth will not utter! Chest will burst!
A syllable — and to the bottom of Tartarus![24]
There are no such words!

Nurse:

                     One.
All in it, yet it of all the simplest.

Phaedra:

Even worse than my death you desire —
My baseness?

Nurse:

             In bushes
Of myrtle — of lips on lips!

Yes! even now! yes! even today!
Phaedra!

Phaedra:

        Witch!

Nurse:

              Phaedra!

Phaedra:

                  Procuress!

Let — go — of — me!

Nurse:

I raised you!

Phaedra:

Proud and pure was I!

Nurse:

Through suffering I made you!

Phaedra:

Shame, which I will not own!

Nurse:

We will hide, we will bury, we will trample into the earth!
We will hide, we will bury, we will trample shame!

Phaedra:

A tree will tell!

Nurse:

We will strip off, we will cut off, we will bind up leaves!

Phaedra:

Nana! A hater of women —
He. Of hair along shoulders
The sight alone…

Nurse:

              The more often will he braid
It, and having braided, unbraid it…

Phaedra:

He will not detach himself from his brothers
Bound by labors and by feasts
Of youth!

Nurse:

        To them day, to us —
Night. The archerlings we will not offend.

Phaedra:

But a worshipper of Artemis
He — like there has never been or are
Of them!

Nurse:

        The higher will be the honor:
Not in simple battle beaten!

Phaedra:

But an abuser of Aphrodite
He — like where yet, when,
Who?

Nurse:
     The heavier will be the payment.
  You will not wake, if you do not sleep!
Phaedra:
  To be older by ten years!
  The wave of the river may not flow
  Backward.
Nurse:
     The purer will he burn!
  All your years — straw!
Phaedra:
  Mother — to him, and by people's reckoning —
  Son…
Nurse:
     And both passion in you and mother
  Esteeming, the more tenderly will he spread the bed.
  As with a boat, so with the bed — *you*
  Will steer.
Phaedra:
     But married! Indeed a wife!
  My husband!
Nurse:
      Not my, say, but our
  Husband! You will render to him for the grief
  Of your sister, of fainthearted oars
  The splash.
Phaedra:
      But the king is not just husband to me —
  Also father to him.
Nurse:
      Ashamed —
  To cling? The stronger will the bond be,
  The more unshakable the loyalty.
Phaedra:
  And what if he rejects me?
Nurse:
  Who? The king, you mean?
Phaedra:
      The king — what of him!
Nurse:
          Then
  Who?
Phaedra:
     But he, about whom…
Nurse:
      You?
  He? All my blood trembles!
  We will leave aside this, that a beauty

81

Are you: above every beauty
A more beautiful there is. A goddess, having taken
All, ordered that it be divided.[25]
We will leave aside this, that a queen
Are you. Not by this did he attract you:
By this, that he in shoulders is broad,
And not by this, that he is glorious by birth.
And that you are a woman of wit we will leave aside
Also. For every sharp word
There is one twice as sharp. In the very
end: power, reason, sweetness —
Even more: pleasure, reason, power.
Beauty burns up in the night,
With her not even a kingdom remains.
As for reason…mindful?
No, always mind*less* has she met
Lovers!

Phaedra:

Then what indeed in me
Of good remains?

Nurse:

The spells
Of Aphrodite. Your man — all,
Will he throw away — take it into account! —
The woman-hater — his childish
Arrogance, the archer — his hunt,
The calling to brotherhood and to kindred —
The son and friend, the suppliant — his altars.
Artemis — that is the whole
Soul — for the sake of Aphrodite!
Of Aphrodite's slave.
So just love then, love
Your own beardless archer.
Of your youth I will nurse,
Like then — grace of those hours! —
Of *my* youth — you nursed.
So that the milk never ran dry,
For two I drank and ate.
So that I may slake-my-thirst-sate-myself —
For two sin and luxuriate,
Enjoy yourself, be tormented.
As soon as you have something — there and then —
Everything to me — entire to me —
Your soul. There is no
Stringed board whose sound is like —
The loving breast. — Your hand!
He is beloved, then?

Phaedra:

Quieter…

82

Nurse:

For what is he beloved?

Phaedra:

Nearer...

Nurse:

For his word?

Phaedra:

Do I hear?

Nurse:

For his looks?

Phaedra:

Do I see?

Eyelids — by intense heat...
Phaedra — they called me[26]...

Nurse:

For his virginity?

Phaedra:

Am I worth it?

Nurse:

For his heart?

Phaedra:

Do I know?

If I knew — in an abyss I'd be!
If I knew — in the earth I'd be!

For everything beloved, for everything beloved,
For everything beloved, for everything beloved!

In this life, in that,
In this age, in the future...

Nurse:

Further?

Phaedra:

Nothing.

Nurse:

It means — you love.

To suit, to please
The young archerling —
What will you wear?

Phaedra:

About that I have not thought.

Nurse:

As if your forehead didn't
give you away — Mad night!

Phaedra:

About that I have not thought.
Afterwards I have not thought.

An unknown country is
Love — like walking in a forest.

Nurse: Friend is here, king is overseas,
Time is dear: take advantage!
Everything, everything, because of your
Timidity — it would be very easy
To him...

Phaedra:
Not that, I'm frightened,
You whisper, not so, I'm frightened.
Even kingdoms crumble
In the hands of the inexperienced...

Nurse:
So in his little ear whisper!

Phaedra:
Indeed even for a whisper I have no
Spirit! I'll look down,
A word — and like the dead...

Nurse:
Why not write to your little friend —
What's being lettered for?
You can't teach birds
Berries — well, alright, —
This letter I will give,
Lips — you yourself will give.

Phaedra:
Neither oars, nor shores!
Suddenly all's carried off!

Nurse:
On the cliff a tree
Tall grew.

Phaedra:
Should I believe? Trust?

Nurse:
Laurel-nut-almond-tree!
On a good sapling
It's no pity to hang yourself!

THIRD TABLEAU

CONFESSION

Lair of Hippolytus. HIPPOLYTUS and SERVANT.

Servant:
An arrow whistled, blood spurted.
And there you go, that's all.

84

Hippolytus: So anew

You begin. — Well?
Servant: The ranks shifted,
The arrow they pulled out, blood gushed…
And there remained for the son no mother.
And there you go, that's all, and Antiope all
for you, green sapling,
Unbending, Theseus's
Sullen wife, orphan mother
Of Hippolytus. Breath — to the world,
Beauty — to ashes, pupil — to light,
And there you go, that's it — and there, gone for always,
Her red lips…
             I have quenched my thirst —
I have had my day — and I see it all, twice
Seven years through clouds,
How with your father side by side
She fought! An Amazon — against
Her tribe, — flesh against her own
Flesh, daughter of the man-hostile
Horde — herself against herself even!
Ring finger with middle finger —
Fight. As in the first so in the last —
Middle finger with palm
Fight! — for three years a woman's
Dolor — a daughter of the cruel-fleshed
Horde dressing herself in battle
Armor — for the blindness of all
Eyes! And each breast
Was severed, and more than love's
Breath passed, one in both
Camps.[27]
        What a fight! what a battle!
I tell you, in that hour
Along the spine a chilly chunk of ice —
How with your father side by side
She fought, as if she had not drawn her own —
By a woman's will! — sinew like a string
On a bow, so wondrous
In flight, that to gods and to men
It seemed a repeated feminine
Breast, reflected
In the air. A wave against a boat!
Too little — with an eye, too little — with an elbow,
With each little vein, beating across,
With her whole (aiming) body aiming,

Man-equal, no, god-
Equal, with her quiver, more inescapable
Than the horn of plenty,
Illumined under the enemy downpour
She stands, not needing anyone or anything!
Bending the bowstring still-more springily
Than a bowstring: with meager-fleshed breast
Leading and so blending
With the bow, so blending it against her bosom,
That not from the string — from the heart
They seem! Arrows fatal-terrible
A so swift rank, a so dense rank,
That — battle or thread? —
It seems: that same arrow always
From the bowstring. Side by side with the cruel woman
A lion? no — had a god in that heated battle
Been — then a god would have been remembered as timid!
So with your father side by side
— With arrows — to her bosom, with caresses — at her back —
She fought.

Hippolytus:
                For my father?

Servant:
                          For her son.

For her chick she strove, broody hen,
For her son's inheritance.
For her son she lay down, the beauty,
For her son's dominion.
Against her people — for her son's sake
For her son's Athens.
She fell — maternal sacrifice
Pure.

Hippolytus:
            I will die childless,
Not for the first time do I grieve over this.
Neither Theseus's glorious race will I
Extend, a family tree branching
On a foundation of deeds,
Nor will I to sons the queen's
Strength — sinew — pass on.
In vain — her strength, and in vain — her sinew!
Giving no cradles, grave
Am I to both mother and father.
But the heaviest grief for the end
I have saved: not a country, but honeycombs,[28]
By woman's blood and father's sweat
To me fall,[29] — to whose
Son — shall I hand them over?

Spit on the childless, fatherless one!
A passer-through begetting another like himself
From the most hackneyed of jades is a
God! as one who has none is a ball
Rolling!

Servant:

Old tune!
In the heat of the moment even a baby the teat
Will not take, but once he has taken it, he's attached —
You will not pull him away! More drunk than a boy
You will suck — you are not the first to run it down!
Everyone has abused it — and you will praise it,
Now upright, but tomorrow lying down,
Everyone has spat — and you will gulp —
You will not remain behind…On a tender little breast
Everything will go right!

Hippolytus:

No hope!
For ring-haired snakes
I hate, as she did — men!
All — suffocaters, all — cats
On mice!

Servant:

So who are you yourself,
If not the son of a woman?

Hippolytus:

Look
On high! Of a she-eagle, and not of a woman
Heavy-hipped. Is it not clear?
Woman-hatred, the reverse face
Of man-hatred, — the line
Is lost! — you with her milk I suckled.

Nurse:

Right, clever boy! (Right, cripple!)
Whether monk, whether reveler — everything from milk,
Everything from the white. *Those*? It
Rules the world. Over all — it alone —
It alone over all the world!
And hereafter, lord, a matter
For your ears — mouse and chink —
For your, I say, ears
And no one else's besides. If a pair were too few,
We'd have each been born with a fivesome. With old
Uncles my speech has nothing to do.
Servant exits.
Bend, lord, your little ear:
Ripened is the little berry, her time is near…
(Hands Hippolytus the letter.)

Hippolytus:

> (*glancing at it*)
> "To Hippolytus — to Theseus's son — secretly."
> Repulsive to the ears,
> That word. A secret? Zeus's temple
> Is built in the open. What is not poison —
> Is cooked openly. Even treasure,
> Stored up for an hour or two,
> Is apparent by its sound under one's foot.
> What is innocent seeks the day.
> — On the hunter the trap
> Does not snap shut! — The conjugal couch
> Is spread openly. An enemy, if good —
> Openly aims. What is not an octopus —
> Openly settles itself. What is not lechery —
> Is done openly. By white day
> Avoided is the blind man — by the wall-eye,
> By his lowing is the deaf mute apparent.
> Earth's depths — reveal a root, yet the root the whole
> Tree reveals. "Thicket, conceal"...
> Innocent blood like leaves
> Speaks.
> > — Look! —
> Be what there may in this letter —
> Your hand labored in vain, scribe!
> Hippolytus is not the reader
> Of a secret letter. Not only do I smash
> The tablet! Together with the wax,
> Wax of sedition, wax of dissension —
> All slanders, secrets, intrigues,
> All, which is — vapor, and not water —
> Boils and does not smoke,
> All which — lips behind a lattice —
> Is whispered, and not spoken,
> All, which is sticky, oozing, viscous, —
> Secret, there's your fame!
> (*He breaks the tablet.*)
> Thus — he who does not know, listen! —
> Hippolytus writes answers.
> *Appearance of PHAEDRA.*

Phaedra:

> (*finger to her lips*)
> Sh-sh…

Hippolytus:

> > In a fever am I or what?
> A woman in my quiet!
> Bare feet, braids undone…
> Who are you — a grave or a sale

Awaiting? Go, dearer[30]
Ask, — you've mistaken the bed!
This is no bedroom, but a lair!

Phaedra:

Just two words, just two syllables!

Hippolytus:

No boudoir, but an ambush!

Phaedra:

A half-sound, a half-glance,
A quarter-sound, the reply of an echo…
Only the glance of one eye, only an eyelid's
Flutter! In the name of the White-foamed[31]
Look: am I really by nothing known
To you, and so quite new
Everything is, to you really nothing in
Me…my eyes…

Hippolytus:

You disturb me,
Shade!

Phaedra:

Are they really to that point
Faded? And yet — I knew it! —
You looked on me so little —
Blindly — inscrutably…
On me you looked so — past!
Beauty mine! As though by a sponge
Drunk up, but this feature, this lip
Grief has not deformed.
Look! do you really for the first time see
Me?

Hippolytus:

Sworn word! As though washed away!

Phaedra:

From an island they call Crete,
Did not your widowed father me…

Hippolytus:

Stepmother! Wife of the king!
Delusion! Crude delirium!
Has it really fallen to me Theseus's spouse
To insult or to offend?
To forget so!

Phaedra:

Not to see so,
At all, not close by, not near!

Hippolytus:

Your new look, this late hour…
Without coiffure — without fillet…
Without habit…

Phaedra: Only with prompting

    Was I recognized!
Hippolytus: How will I atone
    For my sin? But at an hour, when even the guard…
    Hardly without a special need
    Into Hippolytus's overgrown den
    With a shade's steps, with the look…
Phaedra:
                                        Of a drunken woman!

Hippolytus:
    What leads you?
Phaedra:
                            A fatal
    Wound. If your thoughtlessness
    You repent, swear to me
    To hear out everything, with which now
    I break, without interrupting.
Hippolytus:
    Word of a son!
Phaedra:
                        More to the point:
    Word of a man!
Hippolytus:
                        Certainly not a woman's!
Phaedra:
    No mincing olives:
    Word of a man!
Hippolytus:
                        Word of the son
    Of the Amazon.
Phaedra:
                        You — from above
    Have you heard?
Hippolytus:
                        Queen, heard — have
    I. With respect and in silence
    I listen to you.
Phaedra:
                        The beginning
    Was a gaze. On ways without descent
    Was a step. I mistake: there was a myrtle
    Bush — like a schoolboy I am entangled
    In letters! — The beginning was the sound
    Of a horn, which turned — sound of thickets —
    Into the sound of goblets! But what is the sound
    Of things bronze-resounding compared to that from unseen
    Lips! There was a bush. There was a crunch. Having parted

The bush, — like a drunkard astray
I get confused! — the beginning was the beat
Of a heart, *before* the bush, *before* the horn,
Before everything — a beat, just as if I had met
A god, a beat, just as if a block of stone...
— I had moved! — the beginning was you,
In the sound of the horn, in the sound of bronze,
In the noise of the forest...

Hippolytus:

                        If not delirious...

Phaedra:

You — through the branches, you — through my eyelids,
You — through the sacrifices...[32]

Hippolytus:

                     ...You — then delirious am

I.

Phaedra:

  What is deadly is not written
In letters,[33] — it is whispered!

Hippolytus:

                      Am I hearing this?

Phaedra:

For you did the tangled mazes
Of Crete grow me!

Hippolytus:

              That...you...

Phaedra:

Unapproachable — with others![34]
That, beloved, I, beloved!
More quietly than a pearl borne
Within the folds of the heart...

Hippolytus:

                 If only I had not given my word!

Phaedra:

More sweetly than a firstborn carried
In the secrets of the womb...

Hippolytus:

                 If only it were not a son's

Word!

Phaedra:

      I am dead, — no shame!
These stars!

Hippolytus:

          These pits!

Phaedra:

My sapling! My cliff!
These curls!

Hippolytus:

          This matted mane!

Phaedra:

>Make me wise, who am foolish!
>I am jealous of the doeskins
>Covering your cave.
>A sapling stood, with generous
>Shade it refreshed travelers.[35]
>It was I who burned it,
>In a frenzy, anguished.
>Every sigh cost a leaflet
>To the poor thing, — you blush: you do not understand!
>As many sighs — so many leaves.
>No new leaves — life withers!
>As many leaves — so many sighs:
>Choking, smothering…
>*Radiant?*[36] But a shade
>Of a shade! All color is on the bed
>Of Hippolytus. You did not aim,
>But you hit. Like little children for fun:
>You did not shoot, but unto death you wounded me.
>
>But under the marriage bedspread
>Sleep with you for me would be too little.
>Short night, then get-up-and-eat!
>What kind of sleep is that, when you wake
>Tomorrow, and again everyday-day.
>Of another, of a wakeless
>Sleep — it's already spread, where we will lie down —
>Do I dream, not for a night, but forever,
>Never-ending, — let them weep! —
>Where there are neither stepsons, nor stepmothers,
>Nor sins living in children,
>Nor gray husbands, nor third
>Wives…
>>Just one time! Awaiting — I have become charred!
>While there are hands! While there are lips!
>It will be — silently! it will be — sought!
>A word! a single word only!

Hippolytus:

>>Vermin.

FOURTH TABLEAU

SAPLING

Nurse:

>*(over the body of Phaedra)*
>Where is the sleeper? Empty
>The couch. A whisper from the height:

The myrtle bush gave
Fruit unknown
To eyes — oy, juice!
To teeth — oy, fruit!
A little wind blew —
The fruit to and fro.
Always to and fro,
Always back and again.
Who from the tree the fruit
Has the courage to take?
Desired by flies
And terrible for bees.
Unheard of sound:
The myrtle — a body blossoms!
Unheard of sight!
More green than a fruit,
The queen hangs,
And birds over her
Circle. I will not allow them
At her open eyes!
Shoo, kites,[37] shoo!
Agate eyes as food I will not
Give. Silenced
The horn, silenced the thunder-roll.
Always I thought — sense
Of some sort in it, in one single[38] —
But no, look — in her little belt!
She hangs, in her hair,
Like a bird in a snare,
Like a fish in a net,
Entangled. "Cut!
The whole night I await
The gardener. Where indeed
Is the gardener — for the fruit?"
The old man overseas, horn
Has he lifted up, across the ditch —
The youth. He didn't think
To glance at the strange
Catch — it will wait
A little hour — no time now!
Hardly does the fruit last,
Hardly does the bough last.
Och, robber-woman-slanderer!
Miser-dry-veined!
Who with red lips took wing,
Who into chestnut eyes swam,
Froze and stuck —
Be silent, bushes!

Delight there was none —
At least honor save!

Myrtle bush, hide!
Neither to stump, nor to bumblebee.
With *that man's* blackness
You I'll whiten.
Who of old you were — she
Will you be for the king.
With your purity[39]
That man will I blacken.

Whom the gods destroy —
— Eh! — they deprive of reason![40]
For a sensitive girl to fall in love
With a stupid one, eyeless.
Instead of a twosome alone with the queen —
Among the bushes and with a bitch!
Whistle, wind, crack, bough!
…With a savage one, handless!
Not even a beast is flayed so —
As he with my darling conversed.
Dove-lady —
Of a furrier without a heart!
Who of us, me and you — ay, do I sleep? —
Yes, who of us two — who is sleeping?
Because of a stupid stepson
Into the noose? no, a suckling pup![41]
Carve, dark-the-forests,
Into the bough, — och, what gaiety!
How the queen because of a dog
On a bough has hanged herself!
Yes, and I myself — who knows
What happened, came into my mind!
The old woman found someone with whom to join!
With such an oak, with such a lipless one!
Ay, did I not see he was stupid,
An oak? Deaf — stump? Like carrion —
Ay, did I not scent it? Where then was the flair,
Where was sense? Had I eyes?
Before beardlessness of face,
Before brightness of curls,
Before a rosy mouth — the old
Vixen stopped speechless.
But if pleasure there was none,
Yet still honor remains!
Take care, dog of a woman-soiler:
Without eyes was it written!

But what is not seen — the robber is righteous
In the dark! — did not happen.
Take care, dog of a woman-crusher!
Before Theseus's eyes
I will swear on her body,
That black — is white,
I will swear on her earth,
That white — is black,
Reality — a lie, lie — reality
Will appear, I will make it so.
So that in future upon saplings
Chestnut eyes…

Womanservant:

> The king comes!

Nurse:

> …Red lips, he shall not hang!

Womenservants:

> (*one after another*)
> — He comes by the moat! — Into the courtyard he has entered!
> — Who then for the terrible one will hold
> The stirrup? — Who will meet him?
> — Not even a single soul — a wasteland!
> — Who will receive him? — Who will admit him?
> — Who will be able? — Who will speak?

Nurse:

> I. I am bent with tales.
> I will swear on her honor,
> That left — is right,
> I will swear on her tree,
> That right…

Theseus:

> (*entering*)
>
> Am I delirious?
> Neither noise, nor smoke.
> Courtyard deserted, house deserted.
> An enemy in the house? A god in the house?
> A plague has broken out? My son perished,
> Or what? What here is wrought?

Nurse:

> Fate, old man.
> (*Pointing.*)
>
> The queen.
> — Lo. —
>
> But not by plague, —
> By the glance of a bold man's eyes,
> King! And not by the evil eye, —
> By the tale of a bold man's lips,
> The wavering of a mortal's walls,

95

The grip of a bold man's hands,
King! Wherever she steps —
He, bold man! Always he
Is there! Wherever she sits —
He clings, the little shoulders he presses,
The robber, wherever she looks —
He, always he! Neither sleep,
Nor day: "after all, a relative!"
Sleep — he roams around,
Drink — he pours out nearby,
Eat — with bread into her mouth he thrusts,
Into her throat. Chill in her joints.
Drinking-eating she stops.
— Lo. — But not on a bed
Was peace laid for the poor woman.
Bough in the forest knocked,
Called. So on that bough,
And with that belt
To the kind light
She bid farewell. King, piously:[42]
What was woven by me, was crushed by him
Or taken off…
                    Oy, little peahen!
It seems, that dearer than day — your glory
Was! (Little nearby bough!)
It seems, that honor — dearer than life
Was, dearer than the smoke
Of the hearth…

Theseus:
                    His name!

Nurse:
Oy, king! There are no such letters!
To name — the hall will tumble down,
The forest will blaze, thunder will crash,
The flesh of Phaedra will rise
From the couch…Not a raider!
He tramples the sowing — he tramples *his own*!
You eat together, you sleep together,
All your breath and all your
Light, all your glory.
Like a finger of your right hand
Very well-known, very familiar…

Theseus:
My son?

Nurse:
                    You've named him.

Theseus:
                              He?

Nurse:

The same.

Theseus:
>He who was my son: where is he?
>He who has become a dog. We wait.
>There is the deed of his hands:
>*She*. Where, then — is he?

Nurse:
>What — the stableman? Ay, raised by
>A wolf? He's heeeaaalthy!
>No doubt, he pursues new women,
>Having over-ridden your own!

Theseus:
>Father Poseidon![43]
>Old Man Ocean!
>In a black, like the earth,
>In a sorrowful, like the raven,
>Old man — but good
>Was he in the days of Theseus! —
>The lion cub do you recognize
>There, in the square?
>
>I myself would not know him!
>Prince shaggy-browed,
>Roll back your wave
>To thirty years ago!
>Through the rumble of time:
>— Call and I will save! —
>Remember the promise
>Of a god — to a brave man.
>
>Father Poseidon!
>Farseeing old man!
>The best of wives…
>Trampled hearth…
>Trampled honor, —
>Worse than had he killed!
>Not yet an hour
>Vermin has been son to me!
>
>Prince great-quiet,
>Terrible great-throated one!
>Lord of deeps
>Of fresh and of sea waters!
>Support — of the strong!
>*Mine* — in the days of Theseus!
>Under his foot
>Shake the earth![44]

97

Like a stone block across!
Like a pack of hounds on the heels
Of a suckling: to the side,
The robber — but the wave is already there.
With the abyss point-blank!
The piling wave at his back,
The galloper! Swift
The robber, but the wave has already washed away…

While he runs — may his chest burst!
Be accursed, be damned!
May the dogs tear his limbs!
Be damned! be thrice-cursed!

Chorus of Woman Friends:
Who said she is dead? sleeping!
Dressed, anointed…
Who said she is bitter? sweet!
The whole forest to you, the whole garden to you
On your couch, every flower, every leaf for you
Have we brought, the little bushes are stripped clean,
Only the thorns are left.
Not orphaned do you sleep, glorious one.

Now you will have a good sleep, as from the banklet
Into the stream — two little feet hanging down…
Not as a hanged woman from the sapling
Taken down, as his flowerlet
Taken down. Dear friends, we were confused!
Not cursing, but glorifying should there be:
Honor to that twig, to that bough, —
Not as the lecher's woman do you sleep — but as your husband's.

Stand, stand around the tree!
Glorify, glorify Phaedra's bough!
Phaedra's — story,
Phaedra's — conscience,
Phaedra's belt, Phaedra's bough.

Stand, stand under the tree!
Glorify, glorify the terrible fruit!
Phaedra's — timidity,
Phaedra's — valor,
Phaedra's feat, Phaedra's sweat.
Two eternities, two greens:
Laurel. Myrtle. Kin they have not betrayed!
As you "wife of Theseus,"
So he "spouse of Phaedra"
Will remain, two champions,

PHAEDRA

Two supremacies, equal honor.
Sword of courage, bough of fidelity,
Leaf of myrtle, leaf of laurel.

Let us bless then the tree
Of love, planted by our forefathers!
As you wife *of Theseus*,
So he spouse *of Phaedra*, —
For as long as the world stands,
And morning is, and evening is…
Honor to the branchlet, honor of myrtle!
Not mortal do you sleep, — eternal.

Around the bough, which has saved,
Let us establish a new dance
To Phaedra, in memory.
And may it never vanish,
Phaedra's — dance, Phaedra's — steps!

You, fruitful women, you, barren women!
To Troezen's good tree
Let each one at least once
From couch arise in the image
Of her who, without trembling, without rustling,
Both couch and life left behind…
Become dance, weeping! Become a chorus — a chorus —
Not of mourners, but of glorifiers!

Be you twenty, be you thirty
Springs old, be you a wife, be you a maid —
Let each one, let every one,
Gifts having gathered, under the sapling
Hasten — the victory to celebrate
Of the forehead of a woman — *with the depth* of a goblet!
Become dance, weeping! Become a torrent — a torrent —
Not of weepers, but of dancers!

Seen from the turrets,
Seen from the boughs:
The stepson blazes,
The stepmother quells.
Seen have the horses,
And seen has the stableman:
The stepson groans,
The stepmother drives him off.
— Passion my right!
— Honor my armor!
To the stepmother — glory,
To the stepson — derision.

99

In the king's chambers
Flattery with straightforwardness…
— The stepson builds,
The stepmother razes —
They struggle. As her cheeks
Whiten like chalk — he reddens.
The stepson gnaws,
The stepmother fades.
— By what am I not pleasing?
— Begone, insatiable! —
To the stepmother — glory,
To the stepson — shame.
"*All done* — my tears!
An end to my misfortune!"
The stepmother from the bed,
The stepson after.
And had there not been as third
A tree-trunk between them…
The stepmother into the noose,
The stepson — by…
You cannot be bent,
Woman's honor!
To the stepmother — glory,
To the stepson…

Herald:

News,
Terrible! Brace yourself,
King! By the will of the waves
A new cypress[45]
In the house, and a new mound.
Dead — your offspring!
In dust your days!
A wave with a bull's face
The horseman overtook.
The horseman outgalloped.
Steam on the heels
Of the rider. To the side he is
Swift, but the wave is already there.
To the rear, but the bull already sends
Matchmakers, one ball after another
Of foam. Horses in terror,
Snorting, but the bull already big as a house,
To the sky! A mountain!
Cattle, yet no horn,
Wave, yet not water,
Horses…reins…
Best of charioteers!
Reins from his fist,

Eyes from sockets,
Spokes from axles…
Bull or who knows…

Theseus:

Prince-Poseidon-
Gracious-One!

Herald:

     The brave man
Is no more.

Theseus:

     Avenged.

Chorus of Male Friends:

Shall we speak or shall we conceal?
In reverie or in reality?
Lying, and not standing,
Lying, and not steering,
With his whole back
At a gallop and with each vein —
He who in a chariot
Departed, on a litter
Rides, as an old man…
— Drunk or sleeping?
Just now flying,
Now already — carried.

Lightning! Two-wheeler!
The road is narrow only for the timid!
The whip, which he flicked,
Spokes, axles, carriage —
Where? You fell asleep, charioteer,
The cart! Into splinters, into sawdust!
He who in a chariot
Departed, on a litter
Rides, the kingdom's fresh
Pivot — into the lowest abode.
Just now unstoppable,
Now already unmoving.

The way he tended you —
Men do not coddle wives so!⁴⁶
Horses, horses, horses,
Why did they the whole
Coast — rub dry with the nape
Of the charioteer?
He who in a chariot
Departed — on a litter
Rides — is his twisting spine
Bacchus's whetstone?

Just now driving,
Now already — dragged.

We knew already, that what burns
The legs is what makes veins beat!
Gods, gods, gods,
Whyever the young
God-lover from earth-
Rust to the faceless ones[47] in exile?
He who in a chariot
Departed — on a litter
Rides, with whom? Alas, with no one!
There are, but too young to lie with him!
Just now of the same age,
Now already eternal.

A forehead more pure
We will not see — like a marble slab!
Virgin-Artemis,
So you to young
Hippolytus, for his ardor,
Twin of Phoebus!
He who in a chariot
Departed — on a litter…

Theseus:

(barring the road for the body)
Bearers, stop!
Do not move, chorus!
You do not bear my son!
Since when is
Poison of wells,
Creature of the viper,
Vermin — called son?

Chorus:

Since when, king,
Is a son — vermin?

Theseus:

                And vermin
Naming him, we flatter.
Be off, dog carrion!
Beyond the threshold! beyond the palisade!
Oh, better it would have been *to have shed*
Kin's blood!
The mixers of blood
This roof does not cover.

Chorus:

The god-hostile roof
Shall we pass by or enter under?

102

Thunder, and not downpour,
Wrath, and not sobs…
— Shall we pass by or shall we set down
Ashes? But heaven will cry out!
Crushed stone, and not the couch
Of youths: the couch of two fatherly
Arms…Nourished by a lioness,
Then? Even a lion would have wept!
Poison, and not the provender
Of the dead: spikenard, poppies…
— Indeed how gently, gently
We have carried the sleeper! —
With shame, and not with laurel
The king meets his son.

Is he so evidently unworthy
Of funeral cloths,
The sleeper, over whose
Beauty even the stones… —
Have after all had mercy!
Look, in the curl at his temple
A leaflet of honeysuckle
Whole, although dampened.
So also he, your little tree-trunk
Fresh, palace wildling —
Like honeysuckle he flowered
Around the fatherly trunk!

Have you seen vermin — with such
A dear rightness of features?
Stones have had mercy,
But a father is merciless?
Here, come warm his
Cheeks, shoulders, limbs.
That stones are kinder than
Gods — is a thing known,
Noted. They hover less,
Those ones, than they who trample roses!
Let them be kinder than gods,
But not surely than a father's heart?

Servant:

Pardon him who annoys.
But scattered pieces
Into a whole — *the whole* might give,
Instructive, who knows?
(*Gives the fragments [of the smashed tablet].*)
Not accident and not fear.
Something broken in a temper,

103

In wrath, with spasms of temples.
By the scatteredness of the pieces,
By the distance — of piece — from piece
See: thrown down from the height
Of honor, loftiest of fortresses.
(Pointing to the body of Hippolytus)
That one will not utter, then speak *this*
Wax.
      Read then.
To the sleepers — it is known.

Theseus:

Inscription: "secretly."
Signature: "Phaedra."
Signs, burn!
Do I see? Am I delirious?
Inscription. Signature.
That which is between…

Delusion! Honorable! Pure!
Hippolytus's certificate of merit!
Phaedra's own hand!
Golden his tablet!
Virtue's triumph!
Gods, horses, wife, for what?
Grief, grief, wreath of honorable
Virtue — judge over *that woman*!
Hammer, do not fall, and reaper, do not reap!
Son's glory — wife's disgrace.
Snow and tar, pitch and salt.
Snow of the beloved son — dear wife's pitch.
By his height she is low!
Sharp blades into my heart! Wax? Tablet?
Chest — broken in two!
Honor of the beloved son — dear wife's shame.
By his purity she is black!
Delusion! Son! Wife!
By her blackness…Oh, what then
Were the gods thinking, in that ladle
Having mixed in pitch and honey.
Cold of the beloved son — Phaedra's sweat
Of lust…Fingers of the hate
Of Aphrodite! Son, forgive
An old man! A reed of the hate
Of Aphrodite.
(To Phaedra.)
      But that woman…but you,
You entire are not worth a finger
Of Hippolytus…

Nurse:

King, she is pure!
Bull and bough,
Corpse and corpse —
Deed of hands,
Deed of lips,
Of these. — These.
This man. This woman —
Whole family's
Pit — I.

"Well-built, ruddy,
Old, stooping…"
My lure!
My promise!
My aim! "S—
o — n — s?
Right is he who dares!"
I, always I.

"Young: honey!
Young: fur."
Old man, here
Phaedra's sin.
Phaedra's lust.
Phaedra? For nothing!
Phaedra — plait:
Hands — I.

In her lit — tle — ear
C — r — a — f — t.
Phaedra — what?
Procuress — all!
Beloved? By his tail
The nightingale!
Phaedra — wax.
Hands — I.

Nothing, except an old husband,
Did beauty desire, did beauty hope for.
Nothing about the left side
Did simplicity guess, know:
Does it knock from the left, or from the right?…
Cold bed, old husband,
Widower's experiences, fatherly habits,
And it would have been so, and it would have rotted so…
Never upon the rosy little carnation
Would beauty have glanced with her little eye,

Nothing, except a clay bowl…
So it would have passed, so it would have vanished —
If not for my wearings-out, if not for my naggings,
If not for my hidden things, if not for my hummings.
Where to with baldness? where to with old rags?
Braids have fallen down, no askings.[48]
Mangy one — and even he does not demand!
Teeth have fallen out, tasty dishes remain:
Lips–lips–mouth, any delicacy!
Teeth have fallen out, — is saliva gone?
Inescapable memory, a dry thing to gnaw!
At least with someone else's teeth the morsel to nibble!
Inescapable memory, empty jaws!
At least with someone else's breast against a breast to fling myself!
"*My* life — all over!
At least you to your heart's content!"
Heavier — there is not.
Old man, avenge!
My life — all over!
But, striking,
Know, that here
The gods — am I.

Theseus:

Madwoman, stop!

Nurse:

Neither to stump, nor to bumblebee…
With my own blackness
I whiten you.
Sleep, darling. Blow,
Myrtle! By my fable
I — blacker than soot,
You — whiter than glory
We remain.
         Strike,
King! — I want it!

Theseus:

Witch, what for! Procuress, what for!
You — above death-rattles? You — above corpses?
See reason, stupid old woman!

In the world there are mountains and there are valleys,
In the world there are hills and there are low places,
In the world there are seas and there are avalanches,
In the world there are gods and there are goddesses.

Hippolytus's horses and Phaedra's bough —
Not an old woman's intrigues, but the old beat
Of fate. Is it for people — to move mountains?

They manipulate. You? A tool.
Hippolytus's foam and Phaedra's sweat —
Not an old woman's tricks, but an old score,
A notorious struggle, an ancient one.
There is no guilty one. All are guiltless.
And do not burn your eyes, and do not tear your hair, —
For of Phaedra's fatal love
— Of a *poor* woman for a *poor* little babe! —
The name is — the hatred of Aphrodite
For me, because of the ruined garden of Naxos.
In a new form and in a new way —
But always the same guilt is punished.
New lightning, old cloud.

There, where the myrtle rustles, full of her groaning,
Raise to them a single doubled mound.[49]
And so there let cover — peace to them, poor ones! —
Phaedra's bone — the bone of Hippolytus.

Meudon, 1927

NOTES

Ariadne

1. Poseidon, in Greek mythology the god of sea.

2. Pallas Athena, the daughter of Zeus.

3. Referring to the birds of prey.

4. Heracles (Latin, Hercules), the greatest hero in Greek mythology, was the son of Zeus and a mortal woman, Alcmene. Upon his death he was the only hero who became an Olympian god.

5. Theseus means here wreaths of victory.

6. Here Theseus is referring to the fact that by dying at the hands of the Minotaur he is sacrificing his heroic line and legacy.

7. A violent man from Greek mythology who forced strangers to lie down on one of his two beds. He would then torture them by hammering them out to a sufficient length to fit the longer bed or racking them out with weights. If they were longer than the shorter bed he lopped them. Theseus killed him in like manner.

8. Hades was the king of the Underworld.

9. The Russian word for blasphemer is *nechestivets*, the root of which is *chest'*, meaning "honor."

10. Here Theseus uses an archaic Russian form, *nest'*, rejecting Ariadne's statement that the gods are the most pitiless power and thus accepting her offer of the sword and the thread.

11. Ariadne here is referring to the Labyrinth, the creation of Daedalus, the greatest artisan in Greek mythology.

12. i.e., Theseus.

13. Ariadne refers here to Aphrodite.

14. Parnassus was sacred to the god of wine, Dionysus.

15. Aphrodite was born out of the foam of the Ocean.

16. The word "soul" in Russian is "*dusha*" and it is feminine. "Her" here refers to the soul.

17. Theseus is alluding here to Heracles' servitude to the queen Omphale, during which the greatest Greek hero had to wear female clothing and learn how to spin wool.

18. The cithara or kithara was an ancient Greek musical instrument similar to the two-stringed lyre.

19. When Semele, mother of Dionysus, was pregnant, Hera, Zeus's jealous wife, convinced her to ask Zeus to appear to her in all his divine glory and power. Though Zeus begged her not to ask this, she persisted and he agreed. Therefore he came to her wreathed in bolts of lightning; mortals, however, could not look upon an undisguised god without dying, and she perished in the ensuing blaze. Zeus rescued the fetal Dionysus by sewing him into his thigh. A few months later, Dionysus was born out of Zeus's thigh.

20. Buskin was a knee- or calf-length boot made of leather or cloth and worn by Athenian tragic actors. Tsvetaeva's line here means that even youth cannot be protected from tragedy.

21. Temples of the head, not the buildings.

Phaedra

1. While the primary meaning of *okhota* is "hunting," ironically, given the context of this story, a secondary meaning is "desire."

2. Callisto was a nymph, a companion of Artemis.

3. That is, in drama.

4. Artemis is the twin of Phoebus Apollo, the sun god.

5. Pontus is a mythological personification of the sea. Pontus can also refer specifically to the Black Sea.

6. That is, a snare.

7. It is likely that the next word would have been "hand."

8. That is, Hippolytus.

9. That is, not small woe.

10. Some family history: Pasiphae, Phaedra's mother and the wife of Minos, king of Crete, was afflicted with passion for a bull. She consummated her passion and gave birth to the Minotaur, half man and half bull. Phaedra's sister, Ariadne, helped Theseus defeat the Minotaur. Theseus sailed away with her. In the version of the myth Tsvetaeva follows, Theseus defers to the god Bacchus, who claims Ariadne for his own. Theseus leaves Ariadne on the island Naxos so that she may become the wife of the god (and so a goddess herself).

11. That is, a year apart.

12. That is, a treasure.

13. While the primary meaning of *dich'*, "prey" or "game," does not seem to apply here, the use of a word with a hunting connotation is suggestive.

14. That is, count on your fingers.

15. Antiope, sometimes called Hippolyta, was Theseus's wife and Hippolytus's mother. She was an Amazon, a man-hating woman warrior, who died defending Athens against an Amazon attack.

16. That is, without formality.

17. That is, the gods. Theseus is reverent.

18 A river of Hades which the dead must cross in order to enter the underworld.

19. That is, barren.

20. The Nurse insists on Phaedra's childlessness.

21. In the sense of "sediment."

22. The Nurse is wondering whether Phaedra, too, suffers an illicit passion.

23. Literally, "one hundred *poods*." A Russian *pood* equals about 36 pounds.

24. The lowest region of the underworld where the wickedest people are punished.

25. That is, beauty is divided among mortal women.

26. Phaedra's name means "radiant."

27. The word *stanakh* can be translated "camps," as here, or " torsos" or "chests."

28. Hippolytus seems to be suggesting that he is heir not to an orderly, unified country, but to lands that are as disjointed and teeming as the cells of a honeycomb. Tsvetaeva may have found this idea in Heinrich Wilhelm Stoll's work *Handbuch der Religion und Mythologie der Griecher und Römer*: "Thêseus, who was now king of the Athenian territory, collected the scattered inhabitants into one city…" Henry William [sic] Stoll, *Handbook of the Religion and Mythology of the Greeks, with a Short Account of the Religious System of the Romans*, trans. R. B. Paul, ed. Thomas Kerchever Arnold (London: Francis & John Rivington, 1852), 141. Stoll most likely derives this detail from the work of the ancient travel writer, Pausanias (second century A.D.), who notes that "Theseus brought the Athenians together into one city from being little towns of people." Book I (description of Attica) 22.3 of *Guide to Greece*, trans. Peter Levi (New York: Penguin Classics), 61.

29. Or, "I inherit."

30. Hippolytus is suggesting she ask for more money elsewhere. He has mistaken her for a woman seeking bed-business.

31. That is, Aphrodite.

32. Compare with Tsvetaeva's *Ariadne*, p. 85, when Theseus in his debate with Bacchus says, "I – through the sacrificial incense! / I – in the opium of nights!"

33. "Letters" in the sense of "epistles," not "characters."

34. The adjective "unapproachable" describes Phaedra, not Hippolytus: it is grammatically feminine.

35. See Gustav Schwab, *Sagen des klassischen Altertums* (1838-1840): "Often her [Phaedra's] fingers, restless with passion, had pulled at its branches and crumpled the glossy green leaves." *Gods and Heroes: Myths and Epics of Ancient Greece*, trans. Olga Marx and Ernst Morwitz (New York: Pantheon, 1946), 226. See Schwab's probable source, Pausanias, Book II (description of Corinth), 32.3: "In the other part of the enclosure is Hippolytos's stadium; above it is the shrine of Peeping Aphrodite: whenever Hippolytos was exercising, Phaidra would watch him from up there and lust for him. Here as I said before, the myrtle still grows with perforated leaves. When Phaidra was in despair of any way to ease love she wantonly ruined the leaves of the myrtle." Penguin Classics edition, 208.

36. Phaedra is referring to the Greek meaning of her name.

37. Birds of prey.

38. "In one single" (*v razodnom*) in this line agrees with "in [her] little belt" (*v pojaske*) in the next. "I always thought, there was some kind of sense in it, in the single, (yet look!) in the little belt!"

39. *Teatr* gives "*chernotoj*," "blackness," instead of "*chistotoj*," "purity."

40. In English a familiar version of this saying is "Whom the gods would destroy, they first make mad" (Henry Wadsworth Longfellow, *The Masque of Pandora*, 1875: it is Prometheus's comment when he learns his brother has accepted Pandora, the first woman, as a gift from Zeus.) This sentiment has a long history. Something like it is found in the *Antigone* of Sophocles (lines 621-623): "Bad often looks good to those whom a god is leading astray [or, to ruin]," but the tragedian appears to have taken it from an older source. For more, see the edition of *Antigone* edited by Mark Griffith for Cambridge Greek and Latin Classics (New York and Cambridge: Cambridge University Press, 1999), 93 and 230. A common Latin version has it thus: *Quos deus vult perdere prius dementat*.

41. An example of Tsvetaeva's frequent wordplay: "stepson," *pasynka*, and "suckling pup," *pashchenka*, are juxtaposed.

42. That is, "I swear by all that's holy."

43. Poseidon has promised Theseus a favor, which Theseus will now call in.

44. Poseidon was also known as the Earth-shaker who caused earthquakes.

45. A tree associated with death.

46. That is, Hippolytus treated his horses better than men treat their wives.

47. That is, the dead.

48. The Nurse is lamenting that now she is old, she has no lovers—yet she still desires.

49. See Schwab, 226: "Theseus had him [Hippolytus] buried under the same myrtle where Phaedra had once striven with her love…Since this had been her favorite place, she too was buried there and allowed to remain, for the king did not wish to dishonor his wife in death."

SELECTED BIBLIOGRAPHY

This bibliography was compiled with non-Russian readers in mind. English translations are suggested for further reading in works by Greek, Latin, French, and German authors.

Works by Tsvetaeva, cited and for further reading:

Bakhrakh, Alexander, ed. *Pis'ma Mariny Tsvetaevoj* [Letters of Marina Tsvetaeva]. *Mosty* 5 (1960): 299-318. *Mosty* 6 (1961): 319-46.

Pasternak, Boris, Marina Tsvetayeva, and Rainer Maria Rilke. *Letters Summer 1926*. Edited by Yevgeny Pasternak, Yelena Pasternak, and Konstantin M. Azadovsky. Translated by Margaret Wettlin and Walter Arndt. San Diego, CA: Harcourt Brace Jovanovich, 1985.

Tsvetaeva, Marina. *Pis'ma k A. Teskovoj* [Letters to A. Tesková]. Prague: Academia, 1969.

——. *Izbrannaja proza v dvukh tomakh, 1917-1937* [Selected prose in two volumes, 1917-1937]. Edited by Alexander Sumerkin. Preface by Joseph Brodsky. New York: Russica Publishers, 1979.

——. *A Captive Spirit: Selected Prose of Marina Tsvetaeva*. Edited and translated by J. M. King. Ann Arbor, MI: Ardis Publishers, 1980.

——. *The Demesne of the Swan*. Translated by Robin Kendall. Ann Arbor, MI: Ardis Publishers, 1980.

——. *Stikhotvorenija i poemy v pjati tomakh* [Lyric poetry and narrative poems in five volumes]. Edited by Alexander Sumerkin. New York: Russica Publishers, 1980-90.

—— [Cvetaeva]. *Le notti fiorentini; Lettera all'Amazzone* [Florentine Nights; Letter to the Amazon]. Edited by Serena Vitale. Milan: Mondadori, 1983.

—— [Tsvetayeva]. *Selected Poems of Marina Tsvetayeva*. Translated by Elaine Feinstein. New York: E. P. Dutton, 1986.

——. *Teatr* [Theater]. Edited Ariadna Efron and Anna Saakjants. Moscow: Iskusstvo, 1988.

——. *After Russia*. Bilingual edition. Translated by Michael M. Naydan with Slava Yastremski. Edited and annotated by Michael M. Naydan. Ann Arbor, MI: Ardis Publishers, 1992.

——. *Art in the Light of Conscience: Eight Essays on Poetry*. Translated by Angela Livingstone. Cambridge, MA: Harvard University Press, 1992.

——. *Sobranie sochinenii v semi tomakh* [Collected works in seven volumes]. Edited by Anna Saakjants and Lev Mnukhin. Moscow: Ellis Lak, 1994-95.

——. *Neizdannoe: Svodnye tetradi* [Unpublished works: Collected notebooks]. Edited by E. B. Korkina and I. D. Shevelenko. Moscow: Ellis Lak, 1997.

——. *Poem of the End: Selected Narrative and Lyric Poetry*. Bilingual edition. Translated by Nina Kossman with an introduction by Laura Weeks. Ann Arbor, MI: Ardis Publishers, 1998.

——. *The Ratcatcher: A Lyrical Satire*. Translated by Angela Livingstone. Evanston, IL: Northwestern University Press, 1999.

——. *Neizdannoe: Zapisnye knizhki v dvukh tomakh* [Unpublished works: Notebooks in two volumes]. Vol. 2, *1919-1939*. Edited by E. B. Korkina and M. G. Krutikova. Moscow: Ellis Lak, 2001.

——. *Earthly Signs: Moscow Diaries, 1917-1922*. Edited and translated by Jamey Gambrell. New Haven, CT: Yale University Press, 2002.

——. *Milestones: A Bilingual Edition*. Translated with introduction and notes by Robin Kemball. Evanston, IL: Northwestern University Press, 2003.

Vitale, Serena, ed. and trans. *Marina Cvetaeva: Deserti luoghi: Lettere 1925-1941* [Marina Tsvetaeva: Desert places: Letters 1925-1941]. Milan: Adelphi Edizioni, 1989.

Works cited and further reading:

Armstrong, Rebecca. *Cretan Women: Pasiphae, Ariadne, and Phaedra in Latin Poetry*. Oxford: Oxford University Press, 2006.

Beaujour, Elizabeth Klosty. *Alien Tongues: Bilingual Russian Writers of the "First" Emigration*. Ithaca, NY: Cornell University Press, 1989.

Boym, Svetlana. *Death in Quotation Marks. Cultural Myths of the Modern Poet*. Cambridge, MA: Harvard University Press, 1991.

Brown, Clarence. *Mandelshtam*. Cambridge: Cambridge University Press, 1973.

Burian, Peter. Introduction. In *The Oresteia*, by Aeschylus, 3-38. Translated by Alan Shapiro and Peter Burian. Oxford: Oxford University Press, 2003.

Cantarella, Eve. "Dangling Virgins: Myth, Ritual, and the Place of Women in Ancient Greece." In *The Female Body in Western Culture: Contemporary Perspectives*, edited by Susan R. Suleiman, 57-67. Cambridge, MA: Harvard University Press, 1986.

Catullus. *The Poems of Catullus: A Bilingual Edition*. Translated with commentary by Peter Green. Berkeley: University of California Press, 2007.

Dinega, Alyssa W. *A Russian Psyche: The Poetic Mind of Marina Tsvetaeva*. Madison: University of Wisconsin Press, 2001.

Diodorus Siculus. *The Library of History*. Vol. 2, Books 2.35-4.58; Vol. 3, Books 4.59-8. Translated by C. H. Oldfather. Loeb Classical Library 303 and 340. Cambridge, MA: Harvard University Press,1935 and 1939.

Efron, Ariadna. *No Love without Poetry: The Memoirs of Marina Tsvetaeva's Daughter*. Edited and translated by Diane Nemec Ignashev. Evanston, IL: Northwestern University Press, 2009.

Euripides. *Alcestis; The Medea; The Heracleidae; Hippolytus*. Edited by David Grene and Richmond Lattimore. Introduction by Richmond Lattimore. Translated by Richmond Lattimore, Rex Warner, Ralph Gladstone, and David Grene. The Complete Greek Tragedies: Euripides I. Chicago: The University of Chicago Press, 1955.

———. *Hippolytos*. Edited with introduction and commentary by W. S. Barrett. Oxford: Clarendon University Press, 1964.

Feiler, Lily. *Marina Tsvetaeva: The Double Beat of Heaven and Hell*. Durham, NC: Duke University Press, 1994.

Forrester, Sibelan. "Daphne's Tremor: Tsvetaeva and the Feminine in Classical Myth and Statuary." *Indiana Slavic Studies* 11 (2000): 367-380.

Fox, Maria Stadter. *The Troubling Play of Gender: The Phaedra Dramas of Tsvetaeva, Yourcenar, and H.D.* Selinsgrove, PA: Susquehanna University Press, 2001.

Freidin, Gregory. *A Coat of Many Colors: Osip Mandelshtam and His Mythologies of Self-Presentation*. Berkeley: University of California Press, 1987.

Frolov, E. D. *Russkaja nauka ob antichnosti: istoriograficheskie ocherki* [Russian studies of antiquity: Historiographical notes]. St. Petersburg: Izdatel'stvo S. Peterburgskogo universiteta, 1999.

Gove, Antonina F. "The Feminine Stereotype and Beyond: Role Conflict and Resolution in the Poetics of Marina Tsvetaeva." *Slavic Review* 36, no. 2 (1977): 231-55.

Hasty, Olga. *Tsvetaeva's Orphic Journeys in the Worlds of the Word*. Evanston, IL: Northwestern University Press, 1993.

Heldt, Barbara. *Terrible Perfection: Women and Russian Literature*. Bloomington: Indiana University Press, 1987.

Hingley, Ronald. *Nightingale Fever: Russian Poets in Revolution*. New York: Knopf, 1981.

Homer. *The Odyssey*. Translated by Robert Fitzgerald. Garden City, NY: Anchor Books, 1963.

Kahn, Andrew. "Chorus and Monologue in Marina Tsvetaeva's *Ariadna*: An Analysis of Their Structure, Versification and Themes." In *Marina Tsvetaeva: One Hundred Years; Papers from the Tsvetaeva Centenary Symposium, Amherst College, MA, 1992*. Edited by Viktoria Schweitzer et al., 162-93. Modern Russian Literature and Culture 32. Oakland, CA: Berkeley Slavic Specialities, 1994.

Kalbouss, George. *The Plays of the Russian Symbolists*. East Lansing, MI: Russian Language Journal, 1982.

Karlinsky, Simon. *Marina Cvetaeva: Her Life and Art*. Berkeley: University of California Press, 1966.

——. *Russian Drama from Its Beginnings to the Age of Pushkin*. Berkeley: University of California Press, 1985.

——. *Marina Tsvetaeva: The Woman, Her World, and Her Poetry*. Cambridge: Cambridge University Press, 1986.

Kroth, Anya M. "Dichotomy and *Razminovenie* in the Work of Marina Cvetaeva." PhD diss., University of Michigan, 1977.

——. "Androgyny as an Exemplary Feature of Marina Tsvetaeva's Dichotomous Poetic Vision." *Slavic Review* 38 (1979): 563-582.

Kudrova, Irma. *The Death of a Poet: The Last Days of Marina Tsvetaeva*. Translated by Mary Ann Szporluk. Introduction by Ellendea Proffer. Woodstock, NY and New York: Overlook Duckworth, 2004.

Lafoy, Rose, ed. and trans. Ariane: *Tragédie de Marina Cvetaeva traduite et commentée; La resurrection d'un mythe grec dans la poésie dramatique russe au XXe siècle* [Ariadne: A tragedy by Marina Tsvetaeva, translated with commentary; The resurrection of a Greek myth in Russian dramatic poetry of the twentieth century]. Clermont-Ferrand: Faculté des Lettres et Sciences Humaines de l'Université de Clermont-Ferrand, 1981.

Loraux, Nicole. *Tragic Ways of Killing a Woman*. Cambridge, MA: Harvard University Press, 1987.

Makin, Michael. *Marina Tsvetaeva: The Poetics of Appropriation*. Oxford: Clarendon Press, 1993.

Osipova, N. O. *Tvorchestvo M. I. Tsvetaevoj v kontekste kul'turnoj mifologii serebrjanogo veka* [The work of M.I. Tsvetaeva in the context of the cultural mythology of the Silver Age]. Kirov: Izdatel'stvo VGPU, 2000.

Ovid. *Metamorphoses*. Translated by Rolfe Humphries. Bloomington: Indiana University Press, 1955.

———. *Heroides*. Translated and edited by Harold Isbell. New York: Penguin Classics, 1990.

Pausanias. *Guide to Greece*. 2 vols. Rev. ed. Translated with an introduction by Peter Levi. New York: Penguin Classics, 1979.

Perkins, Pamela, and Albert Spaulding Cook. *The Burden of Sufferance: Women Poets of Russia*. New York: Garland Publishing, 1993.

Racine, Jean. *Phaedra*. Translated by Richard Wilbur. San Diego, CA: Harcourt Brace & Company, 1986.

Razumovskaja, Maria. *Marina Tsvetaeva: Mif' i dejstvitel'nost'*. London: Overseas Publications Interchange, 1983. Translated by Aleksey Gibson as *Marina Tsvetaeva: A Critical Biography* by Maria Razumovsky (Newcastle-upon- Tyne, UK: Bloodaxe Books, 1994).

Ruutu, Hanna. *Patterns of Transcendence – Classical Myth in Marina Tsvetaeva's Poetry of the 1920s*. Helsinki: University of Helsinki, 2006.

Schwab, Gustav. *Gods and Heroes: Myths and Epics of Ancient Greece*. Translated by Olga Marx and Ernst Morwitz. Introduction by Werner Jaeger. New York: Pantheon, 1946.

Schweitzer, Viktoria. *Tsvetaeva*. Translated by Robert Chandler and H. T. Willetts. Edited and annotated by Angela Livingstone. New York: Farrar, Straus and Giroux, 1992.

Seneca. *Phaedra*. Translated with an introduction by Frederick Ahl. Ithaca, NY: Cornell University Press, 1986.

Shevelenko, I. D. *Literaturnyj put' Tsvetaevoj: Ideologija-poetika-identichnost' avtora v kontekste epokhi* [The literary journey of Tsvetaeva: The ideology-poetics-identity of the author in the context of her time]. Moscow: Novoe Literaturnoe Obozrenie, 2002.

Stock, Ute. "Marina Tsvetaeva: The Concrete and Metaphoric Discourse of Exile." *The Modern Language Review* 96, no. 3 (July 2001): 762-77.

Stoll, Heinrich Wilhelm [Henry William]. *Handbook of the Religion and Mythology of the Greeks, with a Short Account of the Religious System of the Romans.*

Translated by R. B. Paul. Edited by Thomas Kerchever Arnold. London: Francis & John Rivington, 1852.

Taubman, Jane. *A Life Through Poetry: Marina Tsvetaeva's Lyric Diary*. Columbus, OH: Slavica Publishers, 1989.

Thomson, R. D. B. "Tsvetaeva's Play *Fedra*: An Interpretation." *Slavic and East European Journal* 6, no. 3 (1989): 337-52.

Torlone, Zara Martirosova. *Russia and the Classics: Poetry's Foreign Muse*. London: Duckworth, 2009.

Tsvetaeva, Anastasija. *Vospominanija* [Memoirs]. 1st ed. Moscow: Sovetskij pisatel', 1971.

Venclova, Tomas. "On Russian Mythological Tragedy: Vjačeslav Ivanov and Marina Cvetaeva." In *Myth in Literature*, edited by Andrej Kodjak, Krystyna Pomorska, and Stephen Rudy, 89-109. Columbus, OH: Slavica Publishers, 1985.

Weeks, Laura. "'I Named Her Ariadna…': The Demeter-Persephone Myth in Tsvetaeva's Poems for Her Daughter." *Slavic Review* 49 (1990): 568-584.

Wigzell, Faith, ed. *Russian Writers on Russian Writers*. Oxford: Berg, 1994.

Zeitlin, Froma. "The Power of Aphrodite: Eros and the Boundaries of the Self in the Hippolytus." In *Directions in Euripidean Criticism: A Collection of Essays*, edited by Peter Burian, 52-111. Durham, NC: Duke University Press, 1985.

www.ingramcontent.com/pod-product-compliance
Lightning Source LLC
Chambersburg PA
CBHW070806100426
42742CB00012B/2273